Horse Tales for the Soul, Volume Three

Compiled by:	*Bonnie Marlewski-Probert*
Written by:	*Horse lovers from around the world*
Edited by:	*Susan Stafford*
Cover by:	*Kristen Spinning, Kromatiks, Tucson, Arizona*

Bonnie's other books and videos are available at finer bookstores and tack shops around the world, or by calling 800-700-5096. You can also order books via the web at http://TheCompletePet.com

"Debugging Your Horse,"
ISBN# 0-9646181-1-7 $23.95
"The Animal Lover's Guide to the Internet,"
ISBN# 0-9646181-2-5 $19.95
"A Parent's Guide to Buying that First Horse,"
ISBN #0-9646181-0-9 $16.95
"Debugging Your Horse," (video)
ISBN# 0-9646181-3-3 $32.95
"Trail Riding, Rules of the Road," (video)
ISBN# 0-96461814-1 $29.95
"Horse Tales for the Soul, Volume One"
ISBN# 0-9646181-5-X $19.95
"Horse Tales for the Soul, Volume Two"
ISBN# 0-9646181-6-8 $19.95

K&B Products
P.O. Box 1502, PMB 214
Red Bluff, CA 96080 or
to inquiry@TheCompletePet.com on the Internet.
Visit us on the web at http://TheCompletePet.com

The cover was designed by Kristen Spinning of Kromatiks in Tucson Arizona. Photographs were supplied by the authors and by Kromatiks.

Dedication

Horse Tales for the Soul, Volume Three

Horse Tales for the Soul, Volume Three is dedicated to each and every person within these covers who had the courage to share a piece of their life with the rest of us. In addition, to my loving husband Keith who is clearly the most patient man on the planet!

Coincidentally, volume three is very special to me for three reasons. The first of which is because Colleen Weidner is a part of this book. Colleen is the woman who introduced me to horses when I was very young. Because she was willing to share an important part of her life with a young, horse-crazy girl, I ultimately pursued a career in the horse industry. That one, generous gesture on her part resulted in my teaching hundreds of people to ride, hundreds of horses were trained, I published more than 1000 magazine articles that helped many people through horse-related challenges they were facing and I created several books and videos for the horse industry. If you ever doubted the impact **YOU** could have on the world, remember that Colleen Weidner was just living her life in a generous way and that single kindness has positively impacted thousands of people around the world, including *you*, after you read this book!

The second reason has to do with Alice Johnson. Alice is a very humorous, 81 year old youngster who shared two of her stories with us in *Horse Tales for the Soul, Volume Two*. In volume three, Alice has again agreed to include some of her really funny stories. However, this book is more of a family treasure because Alice's daughter Suzann is represented in this volume as is one of their family friends, Holly Johnson. It was an honor to bring these three women together in volume three and I know you are going to enjoy their stories.

The third reason has to do with my own story in this book. Of the books, videos and articles I have written over the years, I have always operated from a personal policy of never writing "negative" and never sharing any disappointments or sadness of my own. In volume three, I have chosen to share with you a true story that profoundly changed my life. Entitled, *Ginger and Elizabeth*, I told part of the story in volume one, but finished it here in volume three. This is the one and only time in my writing career that I intend to break my own personal rule. I hope by doing so, you will see and learn all the life lessons that I am still unable to find in that experience.

Table Of Contents
Horse Tales for the Soul, Volume Three

Introduction

Horse Tales for the Soul, Volume Three

The book is divided into ten chapters that each focus on specific life lessons. Between each chapter, you will find a story that stands on its own. In some cases, they are humorous stories that are designed to act as a divider between chapters. Whether humorous or touching, these are very special stories.

Because each story comes from a real horse lover who, in most cases, is not a professional writer, I asked our editor, Susan Stafford to edit each story as little as possible. Of course, this goes against everything that an editor stands for, but I wanted you to know these authors and their stories as they told them, through their own voice - not the voice of a grammatically perfect editor. Therefore, when you read a story written by a child, you will know it was a child who wrote it and when you read a story written by someone from the South, you will recognize that in their writing as well.

We have added a new chapter in this volume, entitled, "When Life Is Anything But Fair." While I believe that all experiences have life lessons embedded within them, there are experiences that are so terrible that it may be years and years before we are able to find the lesson. However, as an objective reader, you will likely see many life lessons in each of those stories, even though their authors could not, and that is why they were included.

There is one final *"goodie"* for you in this volume of stories. *Horse Tales for the Soul* has always been filled with true, horse-related stories. However, in this volume, we have included one fictional poem by Mike Beville, entitled "Horse Hooves On The Ground." Mike is a Cowboy Poet and the poem was so good that I thought we would break with tradition and include it.

Enjoy!

Horse Shows And Heroes

Six-thirty a.m., June 13th, finds me backing my Chevy through my friend Margaret's paddock gates. As we work together to quickly line up truck and trailer, I glance at my watch and see that we are right on schedule. I breathe a sigh of relief. I *hate* rushing.

Moose, Margaret's handsome bay Thoroughbred jumper, casually saunters across the lawn, looking bored, and easily loads into the trailer. We pull out of the drive and head down the bumpy country lane. We are off, off to the oldest horse show in the country, Upperville. The show is held annually in Upperville, Virginia, and attracts a combination of local and national talent.

The day is a mixed bag weather-wise, patchy skies with a hint of rain. Humidity is high and the radio warns of the possibility of thunderstorms and hail. Still, we are on our way to *Upperville*, and nothing could dampen our spirits.

The ride from Margaret's to the showgrounds is a short one and we arrive and unload in record time. Margaret gathers her tack and begins her preparations for the day. I wave goodbye, and with my two kids in tow, head to the practice ring where we can watch the warm-ups.

My children, Kyle, 12, and Kayla, 10, are just delighted! There is nothing like the excitement of a big show. Voices boom over the loudspeaker, golf carts whiz by, trainers raise jumps to ridiculous-looking heights, a Jack Russell yaps happily, slick, powerful, impressive horses of all colors, shapes, and sizes glide by, and yes – there are hot dogs and snow cones for sale! On top of all this, I'm letting the kids take the day off from school. Heaven!

The show begins slowly, with no one eager to start the schooling course. The kids and I wander between two rings, stopping to chat with people we know; our absolute favorite being Stewart McGee. Stewart, a former race jockey, (with over 700 wins) spots Linden Weissman. He graciously introduces us all. As Linden smiles and says hello, my daughter Kayla is rendered speechless. Stewart explains to the kids that Linden won a medal in Sydney, and all poor Kayla can do is grin. Linden and Stewart chat briefly about Sydney while the kids watch in awe. Kyle manages a small "hi". I explain that Kayla cannot speak at the moment and Linden laughs, says goodbye and gets back to work with her horses. Kayla and Kyle are thrilled. Now they have another person to watch in the ring.

After having met an Olympian, the kids are having an *awesome* time. It gets even better when they bet Stewart it will rain. He of course loses. He holds up his end of the bet and buys two large blue snow cones for them. We continue the day with blue smiles.

When the brief downpour ends, the course becomes a little slick, but the horses and riders are handling it well. I'm busy watching Margaret go round when suddenly I'm slammed into from behind. "Mom, *David O'Connor* is here!" Kayla breathlessly whispers while frantically pulling on my arm. "He is? Where?" I ask teasingly. As I turn from the ring, sure enough, there he is, David O'Connor, Kayla's idol.

Poor David doesn't realize that Kayla is his biggest fan. She recently had to choose a famous Virginian on whom to do a report, and of course he was it. She even made a puppet replica of him in his red USET jacket.

"I want to get his autograph Mom. Will you come with me?" she pleaded.

"Kayla, I am *not* bothering David O'Connor right now. He is busy showing, maybe later," I reply. She continued to steal glances at her hero and watched intensely while he competed.

Later, the sun resurfaces in its full glory. The humidity is thick as we head for the shade to eat a delicious "horse show" lunch under a tent. We cheer Margaret and Moose on. We stop and find the price on a gorgeous talented gray, jumping clear, is an astounding $70,000. Stewart keeps us company and provides an entertaining commentary on his girlfriend, Margaret's, performance. "Hey Margaret, I could build a log cabin with all the wood you knocked down," Stewart teases. Margaret just laughs in reply. Soon her classes are done and we all head back to the trailer to pack up.

Kayla and Kyle, hot and dusty, dangle their legs off the tailgate of the truck while we pack up. They are a little more quiet than usual, probably tired, I think. Suddenly Kayla jumps down and says, "Hey Mom, I'm gonna go see if I can find David O'Connor."

"Okay," I reply. "Just don't interrupt him if he's talking or riding," I warn.

"I won't. Kyle's going with me," she yells over her shoulder. In a flash they are gone.

I'd hardly noticed they'd gone when suddenly they came bounding back, hopping about like joyful, wriggling puppies. "I GOT IT, I GOT IT MOM! I GOT DAVID O'CONNOR'S AUTOGRAPH!" Kayla beamed.

"You did?" I smiled. "Wow! That's terrific!"

Margaret laughed, "You go girl, good for you!" Kayla continued, barely able to contain her excitement, "I saw him standing with his horse and he looked over and said hi. I asked him for his autograph and he took off his helmet and signed this." She shoved a dirty, slightly crumpled scrap of paper at me. It read *To Kayla, Best Wishes, David J. O'Connor* "and I even got to pat his horse." She grinned at me.

Kyle stood smiling in the background, not quite understanding the importance of this autograph to Kayla, and too cool to make a big deal about it, but proud to be a part of it all the same. "That's really awesome, Kayla, you are very lucky," I said, hugging her. "Now go put that in the truck, we'll have to frame it."

Later, as we pulled through Margaret's paddock gates, I glanced over the seat at my children. They lay strewn in a heap, legs tangled, sound asleep, tired, dirty and very happy. On the ride back home, as I passed the show grounds, I whispered a silent thank you – a thank you I now want to repeat to both Linden and David. You two were kind and friendly heroes to a child in a world with very few. Keep up the good work and thank you.

Shannon M. Gilmore

Biography: Shannon M. Gilmore. Shannon is a wife, mother, and former elementary school teacher. Currently she is founder and President of the Virginia Appaloosa Horse Club. She owns two Apps, Max and Nikki and three Corgis Sadie, Derby, and Pub. She is originally from Cape Cod where much of her family resides. Although she misses her "beach rides", Virginia has a much more horse friendly atmosphere. " It is a beautiful place to live with something horse related always happening!" Shannon is most proud of her supportive family who has always encouraged her to follow her heart.

Chapter One
Mentors In My Life

Cricket

It seems no matter how your interests change, as you grow older, you always remember your first pet. This is true whether you owned it or just took care of someone else's, even for a short time. For me, it was horses that filled my mind day and night.

All through grade school, my studies suffered as I daydreamed the day away. At bedtime, I would sit at the foot of my parents' bed and talk of owning my own horse and all the riding I would do. Mom and Dad would listen attentively, because they knew I enjoyed it so much. I was in the eighth grade when my parents induced me to study harder at school by suggesting I go to a working cattle ranch the summer coming up. I was high as a kite at the idea and picked up my grades enough by the end of the year to satisfy them both. I could hardly wait for what I knew would be a major highlight of my young life.

Kendrick Mountain Ranch in Flagstaff was about a three-hour drive from my home in Phoenix. I think my parents were as excited as I was from the moment we pulled out of our driveway to the minute we rolled onto the dirt road leading up to the ranch house.

After a couple of hours spent getting me acquainted with some of the other boys, I said goodbye to Mom and Dad. I was on my own. The owner, Mr. Frerichs, gathered us all together and said, "Boys, this here is a working cattle ranch. We'll be rounding up calves to brand, so let's go down to the corral and pick out a horse you'll be calling your own for the week. And that means feeding, watering, brushing, riding and brushing some more. Okay? Follow me."

It was a good football-field length from the ranch house down to the corrals and we boys were all down there in a flash, waiting for Mr. Frerichs. He was grinning when he walked up; this was likely how it was with every new bunch of boys that came each year.

In the big corral, a dozen or so horses stood around switching flies off each others' faces and paying us no mind. My eyes zoomed right in on this strawberry-colored gelding, and when my turn to pick came, I pointed him out. "Well, Eddie, you picked a good one," said Mr. Frerichs. "Ole Cricket's got spirit, and he likes to get out and move when you least expect it. You have to be alert when you're on him. Do you have any riding experience?" I thought of the pony rides my dad and my uncle Dutch took me on every couple of years or so. It wasn't much, but I stood tall and answered yes. So ole Cricket was saddled along with the rest of the boys' horses and we all mounted up.

Mr. Frerichs gave us instructions. "Now remember boys, always keep your horse under control. You are the boss and you make them do what *you* want them to do. So ride out of the corral here and get acquainted with your new friend. There's plenty of pasture to ride in here. Eddie, keep a tight rein on that horse of yours."

I wasn't a foot out of the corral when Cricket spotted the open fields and bolted, sending me to the back of the saddle while losing about six inches of reins. "Good grief!" I yelled. "Whoa, Cricket, whoa!" Out of the corner of my eye, I caught sight of a couple of the other boys' horses crow-hopping, and then heard Mr. Frerichs yelling to me, "ride him out, cowboy." I kept my wits about me, slid back up in the saddle, choked up on the reins and fought Cricket to walk. Man, was that fun! I got him turned around and saw that everyone else was still sitting a horse, so the ruckus we caused wasn't so bad after all. I trotted Cricket back to show Mr. Frerichs I was in complete control and hoped he wouldn't place me on a different horse. Cricket was the horse for me, and Mr. Frerichs figured the same thing. "Good going, cowboy, you two will get along fine." I think I grew two inches taller in the saddle right about then.

The days just flew by. I was on Cricket most of the day, every day. There were other activities such as a trip to Slide Rock and another to the town fair, but I couldn't wait to get back to the ranch and saddle up Cricket again. And each day at some point, whether rounding up cattle or just pleasure riding, the other boys would hear me shout, "Good grief! Whoa, Cricket, whoa!" and knew I was once again fighting for control of my horse.

Then it was over. The day arrived when our parents drove up to take us home. On this last day, all of us got to show off what we had learned here. I was going to lope Cricket up and around a barrel about a hundred yards out and back again — a nice easy lope with me in complete control of my horse. Mom and Dad stood proudly watching me nearing the barrel, but then Cricket saw an opening and bolted. Mom and Dad must have wondered what was going on when Cricket and I headed off into the distance with me shouting my familiar, "Good grief! Whoa, Cricket, whoa!"

I left Kendrick Ranch with many good memories. I wanted to return again the next year, but it didn't happen and I never saw Cricket again. But he will always be in the back of my mind and at times he pops into my thoughts, most often when I was riding my own horse that I bought two years later. Nugget was a palomino mare about five years old, young and full of spirit. Many times she would catch me relaxing in the saddle and bolt into a dead run, throwing me to the back of the saddle, grasping wildly at my reins, and anyone within earshot could hear me yelling, "Good grief! Whoa, Cricket, whoa!

Ed Swauger

Biography: Ed Swauger. Ed was born with a real love of horses and grew up with them. He bought his first horse, a palomino mare named Nugget, at age 16 with money earned from his paper route. Over the years, he has trained horses, was a farrier and competed on the rodeo circuit. He shared his love of horses with his siblings, teaching them how to care for them and to ride. Ed spent three years in the US Army, which included a tour in Vietnam. He has worked for the US Post Office for the past 29 years.

Hoof Prints In My Heart

"That horse will never be able to go to a show."

These were the words on my mind as I took a couple of deep breaths, to try to calm the nervous butterflies fluttering in my stomach. I glanced around the scene surrounding me. Although the beautiful blue sky and bright green grass made the day an idyllic picture, these details were the last things on my mind. The smell of fried food in the air didn't help calm my stomach, which continued to twist itself into knots that any boater would be proud to secure his sail with. Kids eating ice cream, dogs weaving in and out from underneath the horses and around the spectators, trainers watching their riders intently - all of these people seemed unaware of me and my impending nervous condition.

Standing by the entrance of the large jumping ring, I wondered what I was doing there. Chip, the Thoroughbred I was riding, seemed more confident than I was. I had been in many horse shows and although the nervous fluttering in my stomach and shallow breathing had accompanied all of them, I had never been quite this nervous before. No one (including myself) believed that Chip, a horse that I had trained myself, could win - or even make it around a course of jumps. The jumps in question seemed to be as tall as my horse and wider than a river.

The beginnings of sticky sweat made me even more uncomfortable, as my cotton shirt clung to my clammy skin. I tried to focus on the task ahead of me. Instead, I focused on all the people who were going to laugh hysterically at Chip and me. Chip shifted nervously, blowing puffs of air out of his nose. My nerves were obviously contagious. His mahogany colored coat shimmered in the early summer sunlight.

His ears pricked alertly; he made a beautiful picture. I had spent hours polishing his dark coat and cleaning our tack. Now it was our chance to prove to everyone that we could compete and win.

Ever since I was eight or nine years old, horses had fascinated me. The power and grace of these majestic creatures enthralled me. Every spare second was spent at the barn. The smell of manure and leather in the air began to be the most familiar scent to me. Even cleaning out the horse stalls was a treat. I always wanted to spend more time at the stables absorbing the atmosphere.

Over the years, my skills improved and I was eventually offered the chance to school other people's horses. Some of these horses would stop at fences or go too fast or too slow. I loved every horse no matter what its faults. For instance, Zack was nervous around loud noises, startling when something caught him off-guard. Whenever Skippy was asked to do something she didn't want to do, she would reach for the sky with her legs, and a strong clash of wills would begin. P.J. was so lazy that he would often eat his breakfast lying down.

Despite the chance I had to ride other people's horses, I still wanted a horse of my own; a horse that I could train from scratch. A difficult part of working with these horses is that I knew I could never keep them and that eventually they would return to their owners. When I heard the thump of their hooves climbing up the trailer ramp and I would see their empty stall, my sadness for having only known them for a short time would become almost tangible. That's when I met Chip. A racehorse until the age of six, he came to the barn with a shaggy, dull coat and a knee injury that prevented him from being ridden. Although he was docile and obedient, I did not think he would be a special horse. While surgery corrected his knee problems, he was still thin and gangly, like a teenager struggling to be graceful in a changing body. His training needed a lot of work. He would kick the arena walls in frustration, sending a loud boom through the building. He was like a child who would throw a tantrum when he didn't get what he wanted.

Everyday, my alarm clock went off at 6:00 a.m. As I would reach my hand over to slap it off, I would mentally run through the tasks I would have to accomplish during the day. I was extremely busy. Every day would be a long marathon where I would run to and from school and then to the barn. At the barn, I would teach lessons, school horses, feed horses, and even muck out the stalls. After this, I would return home to eat dinner and begin my homework, which took up the rest of my time.

Even on the weekends, I would get up early to go work at the barn, finishing my homework at the last moment possible on Sunday night. My school friends would often call on Saturday and ask me to go hang out at the mall with them. Regretfully,

I would always have to tell them I could not, because being involved with horses took up most of my time.

Any pangs of regret I felt at missing high school activities would fade as a favorite horse whinnied hello as I entered the stable. Although I wanted a horse of my own, I wasn't sure where I would find the time for the level of care one required. My parents were unwilling to buy a horse. They felt that schoolwork came first, and anything less than an A was unacceptable to them. Their feelings about this kept me studying late into the night after a long day at the barn. They could not see how important this was to me. My effort to receive good grades did earn me one glimmer of hope: that my parents might buy me a horse of my own as a reward. One day, I rode Chip for the first time in a lesson. He possessed the most basic of training and could only walk and trot. He showed little promise. We attempted to walk over poles, and "attempted" is the operative word. He tripped, sending the wooden poles flying in different directions. Grace was not one of his strong points. Chip had, however, blossomed into a beautiful horse. His coat was shiny and glossy. He had gained some weight, and the added weight made him look less like a gawky teenager. Although he wasn't the most talented horse in the barn, he was certainly one of the most beautiful. I gradually began spending more time taking care of Chip. I learned that he liked to be scratched underneath his chin and didn't like molasses. As the days passed, I realized he was a special horse, and I did not want to have to say goodbye to him.

By this time, I had been more successful in persuading my parents to buy a horse for me. They had come to understand the enormous time commitment I had made to the sport and the sacrifices I had made, such as giving up "normal" high school sports and events. Although I was sorry every time I couldn't attend the Friday night football game because I had to teach a lesson or care for a horse, I knew that in the end my dedication would pay off. Some people spend their whole lives looking for something that captures their interest; I consider myself lucky to have found something I felt passionate about so early. Many people have a favorite childhood place. My favorite place is the barn. I can remember the smell of clean leather, the sounds of the horses munching on hay, and the cool stillness of the barn on a hot summer day. Although it sounds silly to say, my horse has taught me many lessons that will be useful throughout my life. Horses look strong, but are delicate creatures. Even a late dinner can cause them to become ill. The dedication I learned from my horse has taught me to stick with difficult tasks. The enormous responsibility of caring for the needs of another living creature prepared me to take responsibility for my schoolwork and my life.

All the lessons I learned while taking care of Chip played in my mind as we waited by the entrance to the jumping ring. I knew that these lessons would be the important things that I took away from my years of working with horses, not ribbons and trophies. As we entered the ring, I took a deep breath, and I knew that no matter how good or bad our performance was, we had already accomplished the biggest goal of all: getting here. As we cleared the fences in the ring, our performance was far from perfect. After our last fence, applause filled the air, and I breathed a sigh of relief.

On a dewy, bright morning, I began the familiar drive to the barn where Chip lives. As I cleaned his stall and brushed his shining coat, the motions I performed were part of a well practiced routine. Weighing heavily on my mind, however, was the fact that in a few short hours I would be leaving for college and Chip would be staying here. As I got prepared to leave the stable, I paused and took a deep breath as I looked around. The familiar smells of the barn filled my nostrils, and I remembered all the hours I had spent there, the lessons I had learned. Although Chip and this barn were no longer going to play the main role in my life, I would always have the memories, the experiences, and the life lessons to take into a new chapter of my life. The blue ribbon Chip and I won at that summer show years ago was gathering dust in my closet, along with a sizeable collection of other prizes we won together. They would also be left behind. I would only take what I could not leave behind - the feeling of success after pouring my heart into something that I really wanted.

Although attending college requires a demanding workload that takes up most of my time, I still am involved with horses. My parents and friends still don't understand why I continue to devote myself to this hobby they thought I would have long outgrown. I am volunteering in a program to help handicapped kids learn to ride. If you have spent your whole life looking up at people from a wheelchair, looking down at everyone from a tall horse can be an empowering experience.

Even though others may not share my love of horses, I have taken the lessons I have learned and applied them to other areas of my life. These lessons have enriched me more than I can begin to describe and continue to influence me today.

Andrea L. Ponte

Biography: Andrea L. Ponte. "At the same time I am marking the end of my first year of college at the University of Massachusetts Amherst, I am also marking the first time in ten years I spent most of the academic year not being around horses every day. Although I am double majoring in history and political science, I also earned my Massachusetts state riding instructors license this year. The many lessons I've learned from my years of involvement with these magnificent animals and the wonderful riding teachers I've had, played a significant role in my academic achievement and my acceptance to the honors college at the University of Massachusetts. I hope to inspire other people (both young and old) to learn to love these special creatures, so I love teaching beginners! In the future, I'd like to become more involved with a therapeutic riding program and eventually go to law school."

Little Girl Dreams

When I was a little horse-crazy girl dreaming of Black Beauty and Flicka, I was lucky enough to have a horse-crazed dad to introduce me to the "wonderful world of horses". But what do other girls like me do if they don't have family who love these awesome creatures?

Well, if they're lucky, they will find a "horse mentor" to show them the way. Much to my surprise, I became that person to one little girl who had a dream or two. We lived at the time in a small apartment above a general store - my husband and me and our yearling, coming two-year-old son. The owners of the store lived on the first floor and their family consisted of four girls of babysitting age. How convenient! Maybe they could watch our son so I could spend some time with my horse. They were delighted with this arrangement, as was our son, who loved all that attention plus summer was coming and there was a pool in the backyard.

I came home one pleasant summer day and the girls were all excited. They had a surprise for us. I couldn't imagine what they were up to. They told me they had taught Jamie how to swim. "Swim? How, in one day??" I asked.
"Well, we just kind of dropped him in the pool and he started to kick and swam to us."
"He could have drowned!" I exclaimed, horrified.
"No, come and see." So I followed them to the yard and low and behold, they "dropped" my son in the water and he started kicking and swam to them. He loved it! They were very proud and I was a very relieved mother.

A few days later he was having a ball in the pool and I decided one good turn deserves another. The middle daughter had been asking a lot of questions about our horses, so to return the favor, I invited her to the farm on Saturday. She was so excited. We had a couple of polo ponies of dad's at the time – not exactly beginners' horses – but I let her sit on one and walk around and she smiled from ear to ear.

She was hooked! I didn't think her parents were going to consider this a favor. She came out with me a lot that summer and before long, she was helping me exercise the horses herself. If you can ride a polo pony, you can ride almost anything. We had a good time that summer.

We moved a year or so later and she and I lost touch. I heard she had a couple of horses over the years, and then she went away to college. A few years later, she contacted me. She had a small boarding stable and was giving lessons – mentoring other horse-crazed people. She even bought a retired polo pony from us.

A few years later, the next time I heard from her, she was in California writing articles for horse magazines and giving seminars! One day in the mail I received a book she wrote, then another and another! (Of course, she is too busy to own a horse now). Then I get an e-mail requesting stories for her next book – so here it is.

How could I have known that so many years ago, that little horse-crazy girl would become a celebrity horsewoman! It just goes to show you that a thirst for knowledge, sheer determination, hard work and the guts to take chances proves you can make a living in the "horse world" doing something you love.

So all you horse-crazy people out there . . . keep on dreaming.

(If you haven't already guessed, this story is about Bonnie Marlewski-Probert.)

Colleen Weidner

Biography: Colleen Weidner. "I live in Illinois on our "dream farmette" with my husband of 34 years. I am very grateful for his support of this passion of mine and later, of our daughter's. Our children are grown now. Our son and his wife blessed us this past spring with our first grandson. Our daughter is in college now. We shared many fun years "horsing around" at shows. I still enjoy local shows and quiet trail rides; my "gaming days" are long gone. I work at our local saddle shop and enjoy helping other horse-crazy people. My father is still playing polo at 72 years old, much to my mother's chagrin. This past summer I was lucky enough to have another girlhood dream come true. We bred my daughter's retired show mare (half Arabian/palomino) and we were blessed again with a beautiful black filly that my husband is spoiling rotten. I am enjoying looking out the window and watching her play. Life is good when you follow those dreams."

Postscript from Bonnie Marlewski-Probert: *Colleen is absolutely responsible for my introduction into the world of horses, and I will always be grateful for her willingness to share her love of these animals with a young girl who thankfully didn't drown her son! For those of you who are also interested in a professional life with horses, please know that after Colleen introduced me to horses, I devoted the next ten years of my life to working with top trainers in the Midwest, studying English and Western riding and learning to jump. During those ten years, I mucked out stalls to pay for riding lessons, was a catch rider on any horse I could get my hands on, showed in both English and Western classes more times than I can count, and apprenticed as a riding instructor for a full year before beginning my teaching career at age 18. That quest for knowledge – and my continuing quest for knowledge 20 years later – started with Colleen's generosity!*

Best Friends

Everybody has a best friend. You can tell your best friend anything, and they'll take it to their grave. You spend the majority of your time with your best friend, sharing good times and bad.

My best friend was a horse - Queen, an old (but wise) black Saddlebred mare. I knew her for five years before I ever thought of her as a friend.

When I first came to Woodhaven, the barn at which I take lessons, I was introduced to Queen, who was far beyond my beginner level. I didn't give her a second thought until years later, when I was given the opportunity to ride her.

"So, do you want to ride Queen for a few minutes today?" Kim, my instructor, asked. Did I ever! I had watched my older sister ride her numerous times, and even show her. I thought she looked like tons of fun, but little did I know what I was in for that winter afternoon. I mounted, and we walked around the ring easily a few times. "Okay, you can trot," Kim said, and I gave Queen a sloppy signal. Whoosh! She was off in a flash, and I almost got left behind.

"She doesn't like that. Start over and don't push her so hard," Kim said. I gently pulled on the reins, now aware that Queen had a more sensitive nature than most horses I had previously ridden. She settled down into the gait I wanted, and then I gave her a more subtle signal. She started off at a steady, energetic trot. Kim warned me to be careful next time.

I must have ridden Queen hundreds of times over the next year, and given her just as many carrots. Over the summer, I went to Woodhaven nearly every day and groomed her, rode her, lunged her, took her out to graze - anything I could do to be with her. She was 26, but still had the spirit of a teenager. I knew our time together wouldn't last long, as she had arthritis in both her hind legs, so I treasured every minute we shared together. I told her secrets I have never told any human being, and smothered her with affection. I asked for advice about my problems, and she always seemed to show me the answer. Just being with her made everything right.

I was scheduled to show Queen in November, but two weeks before the event, she went lame, so I had to ride a different horse. Queen began to look worse and worse every day. Our rides were cut short sometimes because she would be in too much pain, but she always put on a strong face and gave her all.

Over the next month or so, I began preparing myself for our time to be up. No matter how well I thought I was prepared, I was not ready for the news I heard that January 3rd. The night before, I had given Queen a quick kiss goodbye, because my ride was waiting to leave outside. I never imagined that would be the last time I ever saw her, but it was.

The next afternoon, I came straight from school to the barn, as I always did. I walked into the office to set down my book bag, and all of my barn friends were moping around, some crying. I didn't have to ask to know what had happened.

"Lisa, Travis took Queen to the clinic today. There was nothing else we could do," Kim told me tearfully. "I went over and fed that horse an entire bag of carrots," she managed, and the tears flowed again.

When everyone else had left the office, I did a good deal of crying myself. I hadn't even had the chance to say goodbye. When I finally gathered myself enough to exit the office, seeing her empty stall made me cry even harder.

Queen taught me more in that year than any person could in a lifetime. Now I know to never push too hard, or you'll get more than you bargained for. And that all horses have different ways they like to be treated, and we must respect that.

Queen never once threw me off, bucked, or took off with me on her back. She had a quiet way of telling her rider right from wrong. She was an angel in the form of a horse, the kind you don't meet everyday. I hope that when my time is up, I'll go to heaven, and we'll ride together all day, and her arthritis will never bother her. I'll feed her all the carrots she can eat, and we'll stay together until the end of time - just two girls who happen to be best friends.

Lisa Mazzocco

Biography: Lisa Mazzocco. "I started riding when I was six-years-old, and I am now fourteen. I never thought riding would do so much for me. I can't imagine my future without horses. I am aiming to become either a professional horse trainer or a columnist for an equine magazine. My other interests include writing, volleyball, basketball, and track."

Something Special

It was May 1st, 1999, Kentucky Derby day. The horses cantered easily around the track at Churchill Downs. They all halted before the gate, pacing with nervous energy as they were loaded, one by one, into the narrow partitions.

The grandstand was overflowing with racing fans, waiting to see the most prestigious race in the world. The "Run for the Roses" was about to begin. It was the first of a grueling trio of races that in over 125 years has been won by only 11 three-year-old colts. No one paid much attention to the chestnut in the green and yellow silks. Hardly anyone realized how far the jockey had gone to reach where he was now.

The horse, like his rider, had suffered weight problems, and had been passed off as another dud, a nothing. Despite his handsome looks and deep, glossy, chestnut coat, he was almost pulled off the track before anyone even knew his name. When he shocked his trainers by winning a qualifying race for the Derby, they allowed him to remain on the track. They were soon to find out that was the best decision they ever made in the horse's career.

The familiar cry sounded as the horses flew out of the gate: "And they're OFF!" The field of 19 streaked along the track, the favorites taking the lead. There was jostling in the pack, but the horses in front held their positions until a miracle occurred. At the turn into the stretch, the chestnut colt came up from the middle of the pack, flying past his opponents.

In his dramatic charge to the finish, you could clearly see that he was a grandson of the great Secretariat, a horse many people call the best racer of all time. He powered forward until he finally pulled even with the two leaders, his hooves grinding the dirt, his powerful shoulders pumping. As they galloped under the wire, he was a neck ahead of the favorite.

The crowd went wild, as did the jockey, Chris Antley. After suffering from years of substance abuse and great emotional pain, he had come back. Charismatic, the 31-1 long shot, had beaten all the odds and would go down in history as the 125th winner of the Kentucky Derby.

In his winning speech, the jockey expressed his feelings in a way none who witnessed will ever forget. To quote the man whose life had been a struggle to stay in the winner's circle, "This is the greatest sport ever, the sport of kings, and I'm proud to be part of it."

After Charismatic's dramatic win in the Run for the Roses, his trainers decided to put him in the second race of the Triple Crown, the Preakness Stakes. I felt that I was among the few who believed he could win again. Despite his win in the Derby, he was still 8 -1 in the Preakness. Few thought he could pull off another victory – yet once again, he proved them all wrong.

Charismatic finished almost two lengths ahead of the field, again leaving Chris Antley in tears. As he said in the winner's circle, surrounded by the ones he loved, "Miracles were made to come true . . ." there was a pause as his voice cracked, " . . . and it happened for me today." The jockey's eyes were not the only damp ones at Pimlico that day.

As the final race, the Belmont Stakes, approached, I watched with a hopeful heart. I had seen Charismatic win the Derby, and had rooted for him in the Preakness. Now the whole world waited to see if there would be another horse to go down in history as a winner of the Triple Crown.

The bell sounded, and again, the horses rallied for position as they sprang out of the gates. Throughout most of the race, Charismatic (Care, as I affectionately call him), jumped between first, second and third. In the stretch, he was still trying as hard as he could, neck lunging, head pumping. But Chris sensed that all was not right. He had stopped urging him on. As he recalled later about the moment he noticed something wrong, "He bobbled . . . just at the wire . . . or two or three steps after the wire . . . it happened suddenly."

Care, my hero, the horse I had dreamed about for five long weeks, was slowing, and pulled up just past the wire. I was in tears as I watched the turn of events. I knew that a Thoroughbred racehorse does not come to a dead stop that soon after the wire unless something is seriously wrong.

Chris can't be given enough credit. When he realized that Care had been injured, he pulled him up with amazing speed and agility. Further to his credit, he bailed off before his mount had even stopped moving. After an exhausting race, he couldn't even land on his feet. He fell as he hit the track, yet still reached for the horse before he rose.

"I ran a hand down both of his legs," said Chris. "It felt like an injured cannon bone, or maybe a tendon; horses have very high pain tolerance. So I picked up the leg so he wouldn't put his weight on it anymore." Chris saved Charismatic from serious injury, and more likely, death.

As it turned out, much to my relief, the injury was not life threatening, although it did require major surgery, and was enough to keep Care off the track for good. For weeks, every night, I cried myself to sleep. It wasn't because he lost the race. He came in third, and that is better than most horses could do even without the injury.

However, the emotional face of Chris Antley as he walked off the track in tears was more than I could handle. So, Chris and Care became my heroes, my role models. I turned to their spirit for help, and when I felt most alone, they were there, friendly, caring – an inspiration for all my life.

In November of 1999, my mother was diagnosed with cancer. This created a great upheaval in my life, and my heart was heavy. The one thing that got me through that year was the memory of Care and Chris. They showed me how to live life to the fullest. Because of their memory, I was able to appreciate my life, and my family.

It seemed that my emotional endurance was to be tested one last time. In the winter of 2000, a few weeks before Christmas, my hero, the one who had changed and shaped my life, passed away. Chris Antley was no more.

I was devastated. My life had revolved around the fact that a horse and rider could make such a team. Charismatic, the amazing horse with the spirit and strength to push himself to the limit, is the sole survivor of that team.

Now, he means more to me than ever, and his memory still gets me through the hard days. I will never forget either of them, especially Care. After all, he is something special.

Gerlisa Garrett

Biography: Gerlisa Garrett. Gerlisa is 12 years old, lives in Richmond, Vermont. Two of her poems have been published, one as part of a creative writing contest, the other as the grand prize winner in a *Horsepower Magazine* contest. She has been taking riding lessons for over a year, and although she does not have a horse of her own, she is certain that someday she will.

Gerlisa likes many other sports, especially soccer. Her inspiration for this story was Charismatic's dramatic attempt to win the Triple Crown, and the heroic effort of jockey Chris Antley to save the horse's life.

Magic

Having loved horses all my life, I appreciate the chance to share this magical story.

One Saturday, my friend, George Aiavolasiti, and I were riding his horses on the Mississippi River Levee, when we saw the most beautiful red roan stallion. George warned me not to anger the owner, Eddie, who was the bodyguard of a well-known New Orleans Italian figure. However, Eddie and Prince Lee Allen came up alongside my horse. As we talked, Prince sidled even closer. "What will happen if I slip over on his back?" I asked. The reply was, "I will kill you." Being very careful what I said and did in the future, Eddie and I became good friends. I learned a lot from him about Tennessee Walkers, courage through discipline, and the strength of gentleness. My wife and I were the only ones to bury Eddie, along with his guns.

Here is how it happened:

Eddie called me Friday at my office. I was doing accounting, because that was what my father did and insisted that I should do, too. What I really wanted to do was sell real estate. Ed said Balford Ruff had a great colt in Tupelo, Mississippi, that I should buy. He gave me the information and I went to the bank, borrowed $1,200 and wired the money to Dr. Pegrim, Ed's friend, who secured the horse for me. Thank God, because someone else went to buy the colt that Saturday and offered $1,500 for him. I know I did the right thing.

Eddie and Alex, the blacksmith, used my old car and borrowed a trailer to bring home Dark Magic's Shadow. He was big, beautiful and black. We all grew up together. I leased a stable near my home and started sub-leasing stalls. My wife and I were having a baby every year, and we were struggling to pay Magic's costs. One thing I remember most clearly was getting up early to lunge Magic and give him his exercise. Thank goodness it was still dark and no one was around. I made the foolish mistake of tying his lunge line around my wrist as I urged him in a circle around me. He was full of energy and I was not paying attention. He bolted off to the lake, jerked me over backwards, and dragged me head first through our big manure pile. Ugh! I could swear he laughed when he stopped. Later, I laughed too, and I still do. I loved that horse.

One weekend, Ed invited me to a horse show in Baton Rouge. There, he introduced me to Jimmy Waddel and said, "This is the man who needs to train Magic." Jim and I talked, and I visited him in Brownville, Tennessee, often. We became the best of friends. Jim helped Magic to his undefeated first year in the show ring.

One day, Jimmy called me and said in his deep voice, "Gerald, I have an offer on Magic from Mr. And Mrs. Frank Parnell of Jackson, Tennessee, for $7500." I sat down. I was just working on how I was going to pay the hospital to get my fourth child, Tracee, out and still open my own real estate company. After considerable thought, talk and pain, Tracee came home, Arealco Inc. was formed, and our lives changed for the best. I still cry when thinking and writing about it. Magic went on and continued his winning ways for the Parnell's, but contracted pneumonia at the World Championship a few years later and died. I will always remember and love him.

Arealco went on to buy and lease to some of this country's national companies like General Motors, Proctor and Gamble, Wesson Oil, Exxon, State Farm, Westinghouse and others in Louisiana, Mississippi and Alabama.

One day, in the good years, Jim Waddel called me and said Parnell was going to sell a mare I liked, Shadow's Dancer, a World Champion contender, and her daughter Label's Dancer. I immediately sent him a blank check and our family became committed. We bred Shadow and showed Label, who later won the World Championship Mare Class. Tracee won the World Championship Juvenile Rider Class and her older sister, Trist, won the Equitation Championship.

Unfortunately, divorce followed our success, but I asked for and received custody of our four children: Tara, Trist, Keith, Tracee, and the pets. Our horses bonded us together. We fed, cleaned, groomed, trained, showed, loved and cried together. With the grace of God, we won more championships and owned some great horses: As Beautiful Does, Love Is As Love Does, Delight's Polecat and Kirby's Heart of Gold, Rhea's Sashay Lady – all champions, along with many others.

It all started with Magic and is not expected to end. My grandchildren love horses and are looking forward to their days of continued "magic", with God's grace.

Gerald G. Pfister

Biography: Gerald G. Pfister. A native New Orleanian, has been a Real Estate Broker and Consultant for 40 years. He graduated from St. Aloysuis High School where he played fullback on the 1952 Championship Football Team. He earned a Business degree from Loyola University of the South.

His life long love of animals led to the 1960 purchase of his first Tennessee Walking Horse, Dark Magic's Shadow, for $1200. Magic was sold for $7500 to start Jerry's first Real Estate Company, AREALCO, INC. which blossomed into land and buildings in three states occupied by some of this country's largest national tenants. The Pfister's have owned six World Champions and are now actively supporting Sound Horses.

Jerry loves God and is active in his church. He lectures to young people on making good choices in life. His wife, Martha, reports that he is deliriously happily married, and together they share five children, six grandchildren and one on the way!

Custer

My passion for horses started when my mother sat me on a horse for the first time at six months of age. My first words were, "horse" and the second were, "I want". My grandfather promised to buy me a horse when I was old enough to take care of one. Custer was an eight-year-old, 15.2 hand, red roan Appy gelding with a big white blaze. I was a skinny 16 year old trying to find herself. While visiting a stable with a friend, I found Custer. It was love at first sight; well, at least it was for *me*. He had come off the horse trader's truck on the way to the auctions two weeks before I saw him. The stable owner who bought him said that he would sell him to me for $250, which is what he paid for the horse. I called my grandfather, told him I found my horse and Custer became mine.

Custer, (Cus) was a spirited boy with tons of "Appytude". The first year we battled it out. There was one challenge after another: first the running away, then throwing me by spinning 180 degrees at a gallop, scaring me on the sides of hills by acting like he was going to fall over the side, then the bucking. I passed each challenge he threw at me, (not without a lot of bruises) and became a better rider. I found my confidence, along with some new friends.

Then a magical thing happened at the end of our first year together - we became best friends. Cus would let me do anything with him – roping, jumping, trick riding, hanging off his side while at a gallop, standing on his back, riding backwards…everything except swimming. We tried that once and he made it clear that it was not going to happen again. Cus and I rode the hills in Oak View and Ojai for three years. He gave me confidence, adventure, friendship, and most of all, he gave me his heart.

When I was 19 and Cus was going on 12, he became very sick with liver disease. The vet did all he could, but Cus was dying. That night, I sat with him and told him I understood and that it was okay that he had to go. He died the next day.

I shall always treasure the time we had together and all that I have learned from Cus. His influence, along with my passion for horses, has guided me to work with abused and unwanted horses in need of homes. I have helped place roughly 70 horses in the last three years. I hope to find each one of them a home where they can find the happiness and love that Cus and I shared.

Cynthia S. Carrabine

Biography: Cynthia S. Carrabine. "I have dreamed of, and lived with horses for as long as I can remember. I was lucky at 16 to get my first horse. Today, I have three horses: a 17-year-old Paint, a 12-year-old Arab and a seven-year-old Appy. I love them all and they each bring something special to my life. These days I have the privilege of meeting a lot of very special horses while finding them homes. I am the director of a program called "H.O.R.S.E. Rescue." We help abused horses find loving homes. *If anyone is interested in making a much-needed donation to Cindy's program, you can send it to: Horse Rescue, PO Box 1646, Oak View, CA 93022.*

The Tiniest Rider

Horses are in my blood, or so I'm told. The surprising expression of the equus-loving gene appeared in me before I could talk, and before I could barely walk. The story, as told to me by my once horse-shy mother, goes like this:

My older brothers were enjoying a pony ride at Goddard Park in Warwick, Rhode Island, one Sunday afternoon. My father, who has always enjoyed the company of horses, led the pony as Norman and Brian, four and five years older than me, took turns riding. As my mother watched from a distance, she held me, 18 months old at the time, in her protective arms. My grandmother, deathly afraid of horses, sat in the car busying herself with her tatting. But my grandfather Lessard, a noted local sportsman who knew nothing about horses, was right in the mix, as was his way.

Normally an even-tempered, happy baby, I started to fuss and cry. "She's afraid!" declared my mother as she turned toward the car to place me in the safety of my grandmother's care. "No, she's not afraid," countered my grandfather, as he pried me from my mother's clutch. "She wants to ride, too."

With that, my grandfather placed me on the pony's broad back. No sooner had my chubby thighs rested on the saddle, my crying stopped and a smile spread across my tear-stained face. That's all it took.

And 40-plus years later, that's still all it takes. It is still this same sense of happiness – of peace, really – that spreads within me the moment I swing my leg over the saddle. And through the writing of this story, I have learned that horses really *are* in my blood. I always thought my father was the original horseman in our family, but it turns out that my equus-loving gene can be traced back to my great-grandfather Johnson, who owned a livery stable in Pontiac, Rhode Island, after immigrating there from Gothenburg, Sweden. I have never tried to fight or ignore my love affair with horses, and now I know I couldn't even if I tried!

Suzann E. Johnson

Biography: Suzann E. Johnson. Suzann started riding in earnest at the age of four, but skipped the pony stage, preferring instead the family horse, 16.2-hand Mr. Dillon. Growing up in Wakefield, Rhode Island, she was very involved in 4-H horse activities, which garnered her numerous honors and awards. Suzann took a brief hiatus from horses to earn a B.S. in Foods and Nutrition and a M.S. in Nutrition and Communications. She now lives on Frog's Leap Farm in White House Station, New Jersey, with her husband Art and the world's most beautiful Golden Retriever, Tucket. Her antidote to her job in the pharmaceutical industry is her Hannoverian-Thoroughbred cross, Zydeco. Suzann also enjoys ice skating, traveling, and hunting for antiques for her 18th-century home.

Chapter Two
The Miracle Of The Horse

Grace

The passion began over 40 years ago with my first pony. There was Special, Dawn, Misty, Brandy… but the best of those years was shared with a one-in-a-million, willing, faithful Quarter Horse – "Shiloh," now 34. A brilliant sorrel, Shiloh came to us as a two-year-old, and grew to be strong, powerful and athletic. He could do everything – show champion, pleasure, trail, roping, babysitting, gaming, reining, driving – but he couldn't stop the effects of time. My heart ached over his aging, and I considered discontinuing my lifetime passion with horses.

God has a way of changing our ideas and rearranging our plans for his purposes. Our two grown sons had recently moved out – one to his own apartment, the other off to college. The "empty nest" thing was a quiet reality. In the early fall of 1995, my wise mother phoned long-distance to share with me what she considered an opportunity. Would I be interested in a 15-month-old, purebred Arabian filly for free? "Absolutely not," was my reply. She was a baby, she was a she, and she was a flaky Arabian! Mother thought I should reconsider. I gave it very little thought.

My husband, Carl, kept bringing up the subject. As I thought about Carl's insistence that I at least "look" at the filly, I realized that he missed our horse adventures and trail rides together. We had met on horseback in 1967 when the cowboy lassoed the cowgirl's heart. Our lives were intertwined with the blessings of each other, our sons, and our horses.

Thus began a month-long process of questioning and soul-searching. Was it the right thing to do to just "look" at this filly? Why should I have another horse? What a financial responsibility and time commitment it would be to break and train a young horse. Would Shiloh feel slighted? I couldn't break his heart. A friend helped make our decision when she commented that our horses were not just a selfish luxury. She pointed out that I enjoyed helping kids experience horses – leading, brushing, saddling and riding – children who otherwise would not have had the opportunity. I wanted to share with them the excitement and passion. "Touch the softness of the coat. Let the whiskers tickle your face. The breath is warm, moist and sweet. Bury your nose in the horse's neck and savor the delightful smell."

My mother made the contact and scheduled a time for us to "look" at the "free" filly. But before the day arrived, the filly's owner changed her mind. I was so confused! I wanted to shake my fist at God. "Why did you put the horse in front of me only to take it away?" I must have made the wrong decision. Case closed!

Several weeks went by when Mother called again. This time the owner wanted to meet us. We arranged a time and planned to make the two-hour drive to Delaware. Again the owner changed her mind a few days before our meeting. This was frustrating!

A third time Mother phoned and a meeting was set up. We were not surprised when Mom called again and said, "the on-again, off-again filly is off again. The owner sold her for a small amount of money to pay board." At this point I was convinced the horse was not for me.

It was Carl who realized the Lord perhaps was protecting us from possible emotional heartbreak down the line if the first owner demanded her "free" horse back after we had become attached. The new owner of the filly assured us by phone that he had only bought her to resell her – that she would go to the New Holland auction in Pennsylvania on Monday, if she wasn't gone by then.

That blustery, cold Sunday in November of 1995 we finally made the two-hour trip to just "look" at the filly. There she was – a cute little chestnut with two white socks and a narrow, crooked blaze. At 16 months she was a gangly teenager. Her mane and tail were scraggly, rubbed off due to an allergic reaction to insect bites. She seemed bright, intelligent, and yet quiet. How can you "look" at a filly and not fall in love? I couldn't believe my ears when I heard my own words: "I guess we'll take her." When my check was written, the Lord seemed to step in again.

My father was along and asked if he could buy the horse for me. I told him, "No. That wouldn't be fair to my siblings." He insisted. I resisted. He persisted, saying he'd hardly ever been able to do something nice for me – that he really wanted to buy her – and finally placed the cash in my hand. Teary-eyed, I led the filly to our horse trailer.

During the long drive home, my husband and I were discussing various Arabian-sounding names for our filly. Sort of teasing, I suggested "Grace", because it was evident that God had worked out the whole thing, and it was by His grace that the filly was in our trailer going home with us. Carl's response was that she was an Arabian – we had to give her a name that no one could pronounce.

On Monday, when I arrived at work, a friend remarked, "I thought of a name for your new horse. You should call her Grace. You know, it's by God's grace that it all worked out." We named her "Dad's Lady Grace" in honor of my father who purchased her for me, the fact that she was a fine lady and the fact that it was only through grace that this deal came together.

Grace settled in as part of our family. Shiloh was crazy about her from the start. Needless to say, her training has been quite challenging at times, but also rewarding to see her mature and grow into a lovely, sweet companion and friend. The Lord has shown me that sometimes the very things we want to avoid are the very things he uses to bless us.

Kathleen Davis Anthony

Biography: Kathleen Davis Anthony. Born in 1952, Kathleen grew up as one of six children in Bear, Delaware. She and her husband, Carl, have been married 31 wonderful years and reside in Mount Joy, Pennsylvania. They have two grown sons, Duane and Jason, and are enjoying their first grandchild, born January, 2002. Kathleen and Carl continue to enjoy trail riding together, as they have since 1967. A church secretarial position fills some of her time, but the true Kathleen emerges when she is doing anything outdoors or spending time with her horses or family.

Buddy Johnson

I live in Quarter Horse country,
A breed I truly do admire,
Its conformation, speed and endurance,
Surely sets my soul afire!

And although I own not one of these,
My mount darn sure is a corker,
You see, my best friend and saddle pal,
Is a coal-black Tennessee Walker!

Sixteen-two, thirteen hundred pounds
Of pure Walking horse delight.
But Buddy hasn't always looked like this,
He had been one hell of a sight!

The first time I seen that hoss,
He was inside a killer's field.
And although Jack practically gave him to me,
He thought he got the best of the deal!

For his old body told the story,
Of a lifetime of neglect,
And the marks of man's unkindness,
Left by a whip upon his neck!!

His frame showed through his poor black hide,
He was just scarred skin and bones,
That's when I heard a strange voice say,
"Please don't leave me here alone!"

When I turned to greet the stranger,
Not a single soul did I see;
There was no one in that killer's field
Except that old black horse and me!

As I walked behind him
I heard someone call my name,
He said, "My looks are down-right awful,
My condition's a crying shame!"

"And I have always looked like this,
From the moment of my birth.
And I've had not one filling meal,
In all my years on Earth"

Again I turned to greet the stranger,
But no one could I find,
There was just me, and that old black Walker,
In the shade of a great white pine.

Then he became engulfed by light,
Like the moon on freshly fallen snow,
And the longer that I looked at him,
A deep blue — became a glow!

As I turned to walk away,
That voice returned again,
"You sure look lonesome, cowboy,
Could you use a friend?"

Well I thought, that's it, I've lost my mind,
Like a friend in eighty-three,
And what happened to old Red back then,
Is happening now to me!!

He said "Relax, you've not lost your mind,
In fact, you're kinda' smart,
For I'm not speaking through my lips,
You're hearing through your heart!"

"The master said you'd be coming by,
That our likes and dislikes are the same,
And perhaps I should speak with you,
That's how I know your name!"

"My name is Buddy Johnson,
That blue light you see is my soul,
And to be your friend and saddle pal,
In this life would be my goal!!"

"I'm earmarked for the slaughter,
I may not last the week,
Are you lonesome, cowboy,
Would you like a friend to keep?"

And as I thought on what he'd said,
I guess I began to cry,
For he took his old black muzzle,
And wiped a teardrop from my eye!

Well, I shook myself all over,
And I got my composure back,
Then I walked upon the front porch,
And I paid Ol' Killer Jack!

We've been through a lot of hay since then,
Oats and corn and feed,
And it's darn sure been essential,
To the conditioning of the steed!

We work together while riding fence,
And relax on the pleasure trails,
He's carried me over the peaks of life,
And through the depths of hell!

We ride the range of life together,
Through good times and bad,
He laughs when I am happy,
And he cries when I am sad.

Now I'm the only one who hears him,
I'm the one who gives a damn,
I know what kind of hoss he is,
He knows just who I am.

I live in Quarter Horse country,
A breed I surely do admire,
Its conformation, speed and endurance,
Still sets my soul afire!

As I admire those Quarter Horse riders,
Like Mike Edlin, Loren Grubs and Bill Howell,
But my saddle will stay on Buddy Johnson,
A true-blue friend and saddle pal!

Mike Beville

Biography: Mike Beville. Mike first stepped onto the public stage as a cowboy poet in September of 1998, at Loretta Lynn's Ranch in West Tennessee. Since then, he has performed at Cowboy Gatherings in Georgia, Arkansas, Nevada, Westfest in Colorado, Branson Missouri, The Kentucky State Fair, and other engagements too numerous to mention.

Mike is also a freelance journalist, having articles published in "Rope Burns" and in local newspapers. Mike's tape "Cowboy Stories", was released in March of 2001. For more information on buying tapes or booking performances, you can call Mike at 270-737-0263, or e-mail him at Kentuckyskies@aol.com.

Good Morning God

I must say I am an early riser and that is mostly because of my three beautiful Quarter Horses with which I have been blessed. My oldest is a mare, Dallas, and she is now close to 29. My second oldest is a gelding, Dixie, who is now 23. What I call my baby, Diamond, is now six. It is about them that I write this story.

They each have their own individual background and I was able, on two occasions, to rescue them and make a better place for all of them. I know in my heart that they were heaven-sent. It is these three equines that give me many reasons to start each day with such an abundance of happiness. They have, in many ways, taught me what unconditional love is all about.

It was a strange morning today. I awoke as always and showered and dressed for my barn work. I always feed the horses first. A lesson I was taught at a very young age was that you feed your animals first and they will never go without a meal.

It was a warm morning with not much air circulating and it was so quiet that one could hear a pin drop. I started my chores as the horses ate their breakfast. The sun was just about up above the tree line when I heard a noise, which turned out to be two mallard ducks that had just landed in the back corral. This was by no means a common thing. They landed and started walking around and all of a sudden my young horse, Diamond, stopped eating and walked out into the back corral and over to the ducks.

I stopped what I was doing to observe. I was certain that the ducks would fly away, but they did not. The curiosity that was sparked in Diamond was amazing. I watched as he approached in a very cautious way. He had a look on his face like, "what are those ducks doing in my yard?" Surprisingly enough, the ducks just stopped and looked back. Before I realized it, they were nose to nose – Diamond and the male mallard duck. I had never seen anything like it. After Diamond checked things out, he came back as though nothing much had happened, like it was an everyday occurrence. It was then that I realized again how truly blessed I was to have not only found my true passion in life, but to be blessed with the ability to realize the intelligence, beauty and mystery of such marvelous creatures. They are so strong, yet so vulnerable, and God has blessed them with hearts so big. They are truly a gift from God.

If you ever get time – no, let me rephrase that – *make* the time; it does not need to be your horse – it can be any horse. Just take time to observe and watch these magnificent animals that God has given us. Once you do this, you will not only find peace within yourself, but maybe you can help a horse have a better life.

Share what you learn from observing these wonderful creatures. Watch how they romp in a field, having fun, or just grazing in tranquility. Watch a young foal by its mother's side, suckling or just sleeping at her feet. Try and get the chance to pat a horse's face and feel how soft his muzzle is. Look into his eyes and see the kindness and compassion that lies deep inside. If you do some research, you will find that they have many purposes in this world and one is to bring joy, hope and confidence to challenged children who years ago could only dream about such things. I know how my horses have enhanced my life and brought joy that I could never express in words and I give these magnificent creatures the true recognition they deserve.

Tomorrow is another day and each day I share with my horses is a great one.

Joyce A. Ford

Biography: Joyce A. Ford. "It all began at age three, when I had the privilege of sitting on a big Paint horse. My very first horse did not come along until age 27. My goals in life are to teach others to see the true beauty in these magnificent creatures and to learn as I have the true meaning of unconditional love. And it is for them that I dedicate my life. I must not forget my best friend and the true love of my life, my husband Brian, for it is because of him I have been able to live my passion."

***Epilog:** This story is dedicated to the memory of Dallas, a beautiful Paint mare that gave us many years of joy. May she rest in peace. Dallas died September 13, 2001 and although her passing is a great loss for our family, we consider ourselves blessed to have shared all those years with her in our lives.*

Belief In Yourself… I Can't, Becomes I Can

It's September in Salmon, Idaho … leaves show a hint of autumn. A new season unfolds with bright colors offering a renewal of hopes and dreams. For people of all ages, seasonal changes create an opportunity to believe in themselves… and so it was for Heather McPherson.

During her growing years, Heather struggled with both physical and mental disabilities. Tight heel cords and calf muscles made walking difficult. Her cognitive problems created frustration in school.

"Fat lip." "Retard." Taunting words flung at her during elementary school. "Sometimes I was really sad," Heather said. "I walked away to be alone. And sometimes I was so mad I wanted to sock them really hard." She smiled. "But I knew I'd be sent to the principal's office and he was a huge man…too scary. I had a hard

34

time in school… Math and stuff like that. Writing was very hard, too – my name looked too big and too messy."

A breeze lifted her golden brown hair. At times during her school years, resource teachers lifted her spirits. They opened the door for her to experience the joy of success, no matter how small. As she grew up, another nurturing thread remained strong. It all began when she was eight years old, when a 27-year-old cow horse trotted into her life. Saturdays became the highlight of her week, and Heather and her horse became one as they rode in the pasture. For those glorious moments, she was free of her disabilities.

Five years later, sadness struck in March before the ice thawed. Hoping to find something to eat, her horse started across the ice-covered pond. He slipped and fell. He struggled to get up, but lay back, exhausted. "Later that day," Heather said, "I glanced out the window and saw an animal lying on the pond. I thought it was a cow. I looked through the binoculars, and the animal looked like my horse. I ran to the barn for a pail of oats. My folks drove into the driveway just as I started toward the pond.

I cried out, "my horse is hurt."

"Wait with your mother, I'll call the vet." Dad said.

"But he's my responsibility."

My mother took my hand, "Heather, you need to wait with me." I guess my mother didn't want me to experience his dying.

Another huge loss was felt that summer when her parents divorced. "I lived with my dad for seven years," Heather said. Once again, a single day became the highlight of her week. Every Thursday, she went horseback riding at a local stable. Heather's worries or upsets dissolved as she and her horse moved in rhythmic harmony.

At age 21, an invitation for growth and change came again when Heather moved back to Salmon. Her mother found her a job as an aide at the Child Development Center. "I miss the love of my life… riding horses," Heather told Joyce Scott. It wasn't long before Heather walked down a pathway to horses. She joined the Whitewater Therapeutic Riding and Recreation Association. Life was full … she groomed, cared for horses and made new friends. She became a horse leader during classes once a week for the younger children. "I saw their happiness riding a horse," Heather said, "and I knew the joy they felt."

Her seasonal changes continued to add colorful memories. Heather went to the Special Olympics several times and came home with a first place in Showmanship, a second in Western Equitation and a first in English Equitation. She joined the WTRRA board and became active in fundraising. CDC closed its doors, and Heather found a job in a pre-school program with children from ages three to five with disabilities similar to her own.

Heather started out as a recipient of community resources, and now as a grown woman, she has chosen to help others learn how to cut and paste and most of all write their name… not too messy or too big.

Heather has beautifully demonstrated that with belief in yourself, *I can't,* becomes *I can.*

Margaret C. Hevel

Biography: Margaret C. Hevel. "I was a consultant and reviewer for educational materials with Marsh Film Co., Kendall School for the Deaf, Washington D.C. and Gallaudet College. As a Nurse Health Educator, I was founder and director of a child abuse/neglect prevention program. I presented at workshops, seminars and conferences in the northwest and nationally. My poems and short stories have been published in magazines and newspapers. I have written four novels - the last one in collaboration with my daughter and I am a driving instructor with the WTRRA Equine Therapeutic Program."

The Spirit Horse

Went down to the barn the other day,
Though the horses have long since gone away.
I'm old and gray, can't hardly walk, but still I go down to the barn to talk.

For the spirit horse is there, you see; he comes to keep me company.
I rest on a hay bale and the old barn cat, comes and curls herself up in my lap.
Shep comes over and yawns and sighs
And down beside my feet he lies.

I still remember that wintry morn, the day the chestnut colt was born.
Bold and strong he'd grow to be
And we'd ride and ride, just him and me.

Now I wait and by and by, the spirit horse comes and catches my eye.
He nickers and neighs, and before too long,
I'm up on his back where I belong.

With a toss of his head and mighty lunge, our wondrous journey
Has just begun.
Across the prairie and over the range, up in the mountains
And out to the plains.

Off we ride, away from earth, it seems that now we fly.
I see some golden gates ahead,
A kingdom in the sky!

Now someone else can do the chores as we go racing by,
And view the world from heavenly shores
On horseback in the sky!

Jo West

Biography: Jo West. "As a child, I always dreamed of waking up on Christmas morning to find a horse in my back yard. As I grew up, work, college, a husband and children put my dream on hold. When I was approaching 40, I finally said to myself, "It's my turn!" I bought my first horse, Nickolas. Nick is now 32, and I am nearly 60, and he is happily retired after carrying me around safely on his back for over 18 years. My new horse, Frosty, has stepped in to carry Nick's burden (me), but Nick still goes to our annual fun show and to the local Christmas parade. As a member and former president of the Chattahoochee Trail Horse Assoc., I am surrounded by many equestrian friends. We love camping with our horses and trail riding in the beautiful Northeast Georgia Mountains, and surrounding states. We work in harmony with the Forest Service to locate, build, maintain and protect our trails system in our National Forests. The Spirit Horse came to me like a gift and is dedicated to all the wonderful horses and horsewomen and men who have crossed over to the great trails beyond our earthly realm!" jwest1122@alltel.net

Finding Out Who I Am

Countless hours spent looking for a mirror that would penetrate my armor and bare my soul. Countless words exchanged with friends, counselors and lovers who thought they knew. Countless tears cried over things gone wrong. Countless paths that ended nowhere.

Was I only the product of parents who could not love?
Was I only the youngest of five who had grown up lonely and afraid?
Was I the only one who had searched the world to find myself?
Was I just the pieces of my family, my job, my child, my friends or my hobbies?
Was I only a reflection of my past pain and future anxieties?

I found the answer in the most unexpected of places – in my horse's eyes.

It happened one day when we were intently working on the perfect circle; my conscious mind was asleep, but my awareness was on fire. My presence flowed into his as I ceased to be a passenger and became one body, one mind and one soul.

There was no past or future; there was only the moment when focus was ours. Energy flowed from his body through mine and back into his; I was energized, but what was reflected was me. He completely turned himself over to me as he followed my rhythm, my calmness, my intensity, my acceptance of myself and he merged with my soul.

I can see myself clearly, the inner being that will only show itself when I am focused in the now – aware of his every muscle twitch, ear position, each step and how my body stiffens and relaxes. There are no obstructions in the communication between horse and rider; no distractions from yesterday or tomorrow. There is only the reality of *now*.

I am directed outward. I am energized by the excitement of living. I share with every fiber of my being. I treasure and respect every person, but I love few. I care and I venture into the unknown with some fear, but with the certainty that it will be worthwhile. I am curious and never want to stop learning. I have learned to let go when things are beyond me - I have limits. I play and laugh and appreciate the joy that surrounds me. I need . . . friendship and love. I trust with my heart, but I am learning when it is deserved. Sometimes I lead, sometimes I follow - that's the way of the world, but I'm always in charge of my thoughts and actions. I can walk in peace in the midst of chaos around me. I can be the inner core of the spinning wheel.

I know who I am. I see myself every time I look at my horse. It was there all along; I just had to open my eyes and look into his. I am worthy of the trust he places in me when I see his willingness to accept what I ask of him, his turning himself over to me without resistance. He's known me for a long time. I have just met myself.

Kathleen M. Castro

Biography: Kathleen M. Castro. "If we are truly lucky, a horse will come along to teach us about trust, and a trainer will come and teach us about focus. I have been blessed with both. Santana (Check out "New Horse" in Horse Tales for the Soul, Volume One) was a horse that had fallen by the wayside, but has been the one who challenged me to cross the boundaries between horse and rider. Bruce Graham, my trainer (creator of edressage.com) has been my bridge. Through them I have learned what riding is really all about - partnerships. But before you can be a partner, you must really know yourself, probably the hardest thing we will ever attempt to do. I train and ride horses for a hobby, but more than that, I do it as a portal to find myself and become the person I want to be.

'Pache

It's hard to pinpoint exactly which life lesson my horse taught me is the most important. There were so many: responsibility, compassion, patience, appreciation for the simple things, and the list goes on. When asked, however, the first one that comes to mind is one that came in his final hour; that is, learning to accept things with grace.

I grew up in a happy family, the only girl and youngest of three children. My father had an inherent love for animals, which I readily accepted. I was always rescuing animals, bringing home anything that looked like it didn't have a home. So when it came time for me to look for a horse, of course I was drawn to those in need of a better home.

I'll never forget the day we went to see 'Pache Red for the first time. I was 13. My parents and I drove to Pasadena, Maryland, to see him. There he was, standing in a foot of mud in someone's backyard. A 16-hand-high, strawberry roan Appaloosa gelding, 12 years old, rangy, dirty and thrown into a small paddock with everything from a Shetland to a Shire, all in worse condition.

"All I want is what I paid for him," the owner said.

I rode him in a small enclosure. His neck was so long, I couldn't believe it! "He's a good jumper," yelled the woman, so I popped him over two small fences. Willing and kind, we bought him that day, pending a vet-out.

The next evening I received a phone call from my vet. "He's as sound as they come, good bone. He'll be a real nice horse." So I went out to look at 'Pache once more. I walked down the short aisle of the barn. It was so quiet. There he stood in cross ties, so huge, yet so gentle, watching me out of the corner of his eye. He turned his huge, long head around as far as the cross ties allowed, and gave me a glare. I knew he was the one. I'll never forget that glare, so stoic, saying, "Hello, it's me, I'm here," as if we had known one another in a past life.

I boarded 'Pache at the barn where I had been taking lessons since the age of five. The other students were winning local and regional shows on flashy bay horses. I didn't care; I happily brought my strawberry roan Appaloosa into the barn. Stares and comments didn't bother me, even at that young age when fitting in was so important.

I rode 'Pache Red every day and competed in some local shows. He was a solid horse, a good jumper, and he loved people. An easy keeper with a tremendous personality, he seemed to like his new surroundings. I was so intimidated by him at times, though, because he would try to take off to the barn from the trails when I wasn't paying attention. He would always give me a warning first, however; a flash of the white of his eye, as if to say, "If you're not paying attention, I'm going!"

The days riding 'Pache with my friend Mika and her horse, Flashdance, were so much fun. We talked about everything from boys to school on our long trail rides, the horses moving their ears back and forth as if really listening.

Time passed and I went on to college. Mika and I moved both horses to another stable called Paradise Farms. What a perfect name. It was a beautiful farm, hundreds of years old, but extremely well kept. A happy place.

Both the farm and my horse are gone now, leaving vivid memories of happier times, and of what happened one overcast day in July of 1991. What I gained that day cannot be measured against any other hardship that has happened in my life. What happened that day prepared me, literally, for life.

Two years before, a cancerous tumor had grown on 'Pache's eyelid. We sent him to New Bolton, Pennsylvania, for its removal. The cancer was also found in his lymph nodes, and the vets gave him about two years to live.

The doctors were right. In December, 1990, he started having trouble breathing and grew a large mass in his chest. But he seemed happy, retired in the field with his pasture mates. The vet and I both agreed that surgery was not a humane option. Putting an 18-year-old horse through surgery with an unknown mass around his heart would likely be cruel and too risky. In January of 1991, another tumor grew on his eyelid that caused 'Pache to lose his eye, and his life.

While on a family vacation in July of that same year, I received a call from the barn manager telling me to come home immediately. I knew it was something terrible. 'Pache had scratched an eye out in the field.

I arrived home and Mika was so kind to take me to see him. 'Pache was standing in his stall, one-eyed and in pain. The vet was there and said, "I'm sorry, it is best to put him down". The words didn't shock me. I was already prepared for the worst. We scheduled the euthanization and the vet left.

While Mika talked to the barn manager outside, I explained to 'Pache what was happening. He seemed to listen intently. As I cut off a lock of his strawberry-colored tail which matched my hair exactly, he watched me with his good eye. It was as if he was glad I had thought to save a treasure from a best friend.

The next morning was overcast. Mika picked me up at home. As I left, my mom, tears welling in her eyes, said she would be waiting for me when I returned. And so I went to do the dreaded deed that only animal owners can understand.

As I walked to get 'Pache in the field, I was fumbling with his halter, memories flashing through my mind. I looked up to find him already coming toward me, so calm, so selective about where he was placing his feet. He looked so white that day, so angelic.

I let him graze while everyone prepared. As the vet's assistant came over to take him, everything became slow motion. I ran my hand from his forehead to his rump and told him to "go on… it's okay… goodbye 'Pache." She took hold of the lead from my hand and 'Pache turned his head to go with her, but didn't budge his body. He had never done that! He had always gone with the handler. It was as if he was saying, "no wait, just a little bit more time." I gently pushed his head away and said, "Go."

With his good eye toward me, he took a few steps and gave me a glare just like he gave me in the barn years earlier when in cross ties. Time stood still; I saw into his soul. My heart sank so low, I felt numb. He had trusted me for so long, and was trusting me that this, too, would be okay. Or was I the one that needed the comfort? I felt that he was saying *goodbye, thank you*, so gracefully, just as he had many years earlier said, *hello, I'm here.*

I followed him to the patch of grass outside the paddock designated for him to rest. All of his pasture mates stood quietly by the fence, staying by him until the very end. The vet commented, "This is normal, they always seem to know." I then patted 'Pache on the neck, kissed his warm face and, holding back tears, turned with Mika and walked up over the hill. I looked back and there he stood, calm, knowing, so obedient for the vet and assistant.

Shortly thereafter, the vet assistant came slowly walking over the hill to where Mika and I stood. Carrying his "empty" halter, still with white hairs in it, she said, "It's all over, it was real fast." Suddenly, the sun broke through the clouds. The day then seemed glorious.

That day, 'Pache taught me one of life's most important lessons – to accept things with grace. Since that day, I have learned that I have a chronic illness, my father died a tragic death in a car accident, my dear grandmother died, I put down my 19-year-old dog, and my mother developed breast cancer. All were much easier for me to handle and accept because of that one look given to me by my horse in his last moments here on Earth. 'Pache knew and he accepted it, saying only *thank you* and *everything will be okay.*

Kristen Amacher Zeman

Biography: Kristen Amacher Zeman. Kristen's passion for horses and dogs began at a very early age. A multiple award winner for her art, poetry and stories, Kristen currently resides in Maryland with her husband and extended family of horses and dogs. She remains an avid rider and rescuer of horses. A few years back, she started a photography business, namely ©Kristen Amacher Zeman photography and ©KAZ Creations, focusing mainly on black and white photos of dogs and horses. Her work can be found in shops in areas such as Middleburg, Virginia and Baltimore, Maryland. With her website currently under construction, Kristen welcomes e-mails at kzeman1@aol.com.

Possy's Cart Ride

Here she comes. She has my halter and lead rope and that dopey grin she gets whenever it's time to pull that heavy box on wheels all over the hills, over the hard black top, through this scary forest and back to my sanctuary, my stall. She calls it "driving", but I call it hard work. I pull this box of hers, with her and her dog in it, for miles and miles at a crisp trot and she has the nerve to sing the whole time. I know I'm complaining, but it's not all bad. It all starts out with a good scratching all over with a currycomb.

Of course, she ties me up good and tight so I can't sneak any of the tender blades of grass growing along the fence line. Then she gets an assortment of delicious brushes and starts at my poll and finishes below my perfect hocks. She spends extra time scratching my withers, which I find heavenly. All of this wondrous pleasure comes to an abrupt halt when she insists on slapping on that mass of cowhide straps that she calls a harness. The part I hate the most is that nasty strap she sticks right under my tail! Of all the nerve!

Oh well, with all that over with, I'm beginning to feel like a bit of exercise after all. Hurry up, let's go! She growls at me to stay put while she wraps the poles that trap my gorgeous body to that box. (Some think I have a big ego, but I prefer to call it great self-esteem).

Finally, she gets in the box/cart, whatever it's called, and off we go! There are a lot of scary people-movers (cars) between the barn and the trail, but I try to be brave. After all, I was a stallion for 16 of my 29 years and I still have lots of moxy. Oh no, here comes a huge people-mover with those noisy air sounds when it stops (trash tuck)! The very ground I walk on shook as it passed within inches of my sleek form, but I did not panic. I have grown to trust the girl. Besides, I come from a very solid old line of Morgan horses and would hate to embarrass my relatives with stories of explosions or loss of mind.

Having made it past the noisy people-mover in one piece, I see the groomed, soft trail up ahead. This is where the girl's insatiable desire for speed takes over. She's taking up the reins and clucking, which means she wants a big, high trot with tons of motion. Okay, okay, she wants even bigger action from my front end. No need to use that nasty whip, I get the picture. Her demands at time are a little beyond my years; however, I usually enjoy the challenge. In fact today, I'm loving it.

Now she wants me to canter through the tunnel, which we both know is a bad idea, but unfortunately, I am not in charge. My desire to buck is almost overwhelming, but my years of formal training have guilted me out of it. It turns out to be a good thing, because right smack in the middle of the tunnel we almost literally run into a bug-eyed filly with an owner to match. They seem to be looking at me and my box as some kind of equine devouring monstrosity. We quickly stop and let the silly willies go by, snorting and bending as far around as they possibly can. I secretly chuckle, though I know it's not kind.

After the tunnel, we encounter several more of my kind and their less-than-in-charge riders, but I'm in a generous mood and do not make any sudden moves to add humor to what I think is almost funny. After all, we were all young once.

Back to the business of enjoying ourselves. My girl yells, "road trot", and we are off and flying again. I lift my noble head to inhale the cool smell of eucalyptus trees as I almost float down the trail. Soon, the enjoyment ends, however, since my young master can never get enough, and yells, "Trot-on!" This means fly – practically – and so I do. The dirt clods flying from my feet become lethal weapons as I gather all the significant power I have left and give it my best. Just when my lungs are aching and I think walking might be fun, the girl seems to read my mind and asks me to slow down. She does have a heart after all. Still I pull the bit, showing some resistance to slowing down, but it's all just for show.

Happily, after all this fast pace, she lets me walk the last two miles back to the barn. Whenever she seems to be daydreaming, I snatch a bite of grass that grows along the trail and devour it as fast as I can. This little game delights me to no end; however, it seems to irritate the girl a great deal. (Maybe that's the appeal?) After about the third bite, she uses the whip on my backside just enough to get her point across. The game is over.

When I see my home on the horizon, I get a little anxious and want to trot again, but she insists we walk. She probably knows what's best. Once home, I get to relax again. The girl removes all the itchy cowhide and gives me a thorough brushing or, if it's hot, a cool bath. Then she returns me to my stall where I blissfully roll while she looks on with this disgusted face. I don't think people like dirt much. They don't seem to appreciate the joy of a good roll and I never see them scratch their faces on fence posts. Before it is dark, she puts a blanket on me, feeds me my grass hay and oats, checks my water and gives me this funny smacking on the face. I really don't know what that is about, but something about it feels good, and I allow it. After all, she did bring the oats! I sleep blissfully, dreaming about future cart rides and the next good scratching.

Glenna Cresci

Biography: Glenna Cresci. "I grew up in Los Angeles, California, begging for a horse from the time I could talk. We eventually moved where I could indulge my passion for horses, buying my first mare, a part-Morgan named Sham. I moved into the hunter/jumper and Thoroughbred world in my teens, but came back to Morgan horses as an adult. I took up carriage driving 15 years ago with the purchase of Poseidon, my dream horse, who is now 30 years old. Driving him has been the most fun I have ever had and it has given me the "driving bug" forever."

Chapter Three
The Intelligence Of The Horse

Prince Twist

Our first registered horse was a three-year-old leopard Appaloosa stallion named Prince Twist. We knew that stallions were "different", but we had no idea how different ours would be.

He had a couple of faults, though, as every horse does. That's why breeders keep breeding to improve – to get the "perfect horse". Twist was very heavily muscled, but a little on the "short" side. He also had just one eye. The other had been lost in an accident when he was a yearling. From the time we had him until the day he died, we compensated for this "fault" of his. Whenever he was led anywhere we said "up" and he would know that there was some sort of obstacle to step over or down.

Luckily for us, he had an extremely sweet disposition. In his first winter with us, he somehow escaped from his stall and went on a barn tour. When our six-year-old son came to the house and reported that "Twist was out", we flew into action, only to have him say "It's okay. I put him back." Twist later became a babysitter to our daughter. I usually took the kids to the barn to do chores and the safest place for my two-year-old was on the back of Twist, sitting on his blanket and counting spots as only a little girl can.

He was easy to breed and we learned how to back him off a mare if things weren't just quite right. He proved to be an exceptional sire and his get won prestigious shows in Ontario and the USA. Our proudest moment was when a weanling filly by Twist won the World Championship Show in Oklahoma! First out of 86 fillies shown! That was just our third foal from him. Talk about lots of laughter and tears!

Twist was shown in Western Pleasure and in his first show, placed second out of 82 horses at the 1977 U.S. National Show in Syracuse. The next year, I showed him in Ontario shows (after I learned how to ride) and we were high point many times. He was almost a "push-button" horse. He would change direction or gait with just a light shift in my weight or a word softly spoken. Judges never spotted his "socket", partly because his white forelock was very long and hung almost completely over that entire side of his face.

Then one day, a friend dropped by and, looking into his only eye, thought that Twist may be developing cataracts. I wondered why he had been stumbling a bit when I rode him in the outside pen....! For quite some time after that I didn't ride him. I would

exercise him by either putting him out with the mares in the pasture – except they would wander off from his "bad" side and he wouldn't notice for a while and then be really annoyed when he discovered they were on the other side of the field! The only other way to exercise him was to turn him loose in the paddock and holler "WHOA!" for him to avoid hitting the fence at a gallop. He'd do a sliding stop that would impress many a reiner, wheel around and race in another direction until he responded to your next command.

He was, though, becoming almost totally blind. His good eye was becoming "sympathetic" to his lost eye. We booked an ophthalmologist appointment for him, because we couldn't bear to think of him suffering. The day of his appointment I led him to the trailer, threw the lead rope over his neck, said "up" and in he went, just like he had done dozens of times before. My dad came along for the two-hour drive to keep me company, even though he knew nothing about horses.

The doctor was very kind and quite impressed by how quiet this now 15-year-old stallion was. Not a surprise to all who knew him! Part of his examination included a "test run" through an obstacle course in a dark barn. The vet instructed me to walk around the barn and not say a word to Twist. After a few minutes of this torture I was in tears because he, naturally, failed every single obstacle. Every time his foot hit something or he stumbled I would sob more. It was one of the most difficult things I had ever had to do. At the completion of the course, the vet was shaking his head sadly. We had failed miserably! I asked if I could please try it again. He must have either thought I was a complete idiot or felt extremely sorry for me, because he let me lead him through one more time.

This time Twist didn't hit one single thing! He didn't stumble or trip and fall. We were, just like long ago, perfect!

The vet was grinning and so was I by the time we finished. He asked what my secret was. I told him about our word "up" and how Twist knew what to do when he heard that one little word. How proud I was of our boy!

The sad part was that surgery wasn't feasible. Twist's chances of improved sight and recovery from surgery were slim. I was still crying when I went to load him for our return trip home and hesitated when I realized he couldn't see where he was going! The vet said to "just keep doing what you've been doing for him for all these years. Your family has been his 'eyes' for so long now that the trust he has learned is going to be enough for him to 'see' for the rest of his life."

47

Twist lived for nearly two more years before we had to put him down because of an impacted bowel. I still get teary-eyed when I think of him. He taught us *so* much about trust and love. We will never forget him!

Anne Marie Szebedinszky

Biography: Anne Marie Szebedinszky. Anne and husband Frank live near Port Perry, Ontario. Parents of two children and grandparents to twins, they have been breeding, fitting and showing world-class halter and performance horses since 1977. Some of their successes have included a World Champion filly and numerous Futurity winners. They now spend most of the show season fitting and showing Quarter Horses for clients - with very impressive results!

Beautiful Hearts

How gently can a horse touch the heart of a child? Like the tickle of a feather not really noticed at first, but the presence there and softly reaching out to caress the soul. My daughter Christie had been with horses since she was able to breathe. When she was a wee babe, her time was spent in a playpen at ringside. As soon as she could sit up, maybe even before, Christie was on a horse. Sunday mornings would find her competing in the local lead line classes, the spectators taken with the love and trust between the little girl and her mare. Ah, she rode a special little mare, and was always quick to groom her, help feed her or clean the stall. Horse treats were never forgotten. The child was riding on her own at four years old, a bond between horse and rider that came easy. She hurried home from school just to ride, and everyone in the class knew Sable by name.

Christie's nights were spent dreaming about the next show. The training for youth classes was going well. Instead of lead line, plans were going well for advancement including showmanship, pleasure and trail classes. Sable was learning to back an "L"' for Christie.

Together, my daughter and I had chosen a stallion and planned to breed Sable. Christie was so much looking forward to the baby. She could picture a little foal dancing around the field with her and wanted it to be a filly that she could help train and show. To Christie, loving that little mare was something that was as sure as the sunrise. But how quickly things can change. One dark February night the mare colicked and was gone.

How do you tell a little girl she won't see her friend any more? How do you take a heart and mend it when you have no thread? It's hell explaining death to a child, especially when it is so sudden and unexpected. I didn't understand it myself. We entered the barn early one morning as usual. Sable nickered when she heard us but she was down, her breathing irregular. As she lay back into the straw something was drastically wrong. Christie didn't understand what was happening and at that point, neither did I. My daughter wanted to come close, but I wouldn't let her for fear Sable would struggle and injure her. I didn't realize the mare was dying. My mind was in such turmoil; Christie was rushed off, the vet came. We tried to keep Sable warm but there was no helping her, so with her head in my lap, she made her final journey. Christie never had the chance to give her friend one last pat.

I told her that horses get sick and even though the vet tried, her horse couldn't be helped. I explained that Sable had gone to heaven to be with Grandpa. Christie wanted to know why her mare had gotten sick. What had killed her? How could I tell her a tummy ache had caused a death? So many questions from a little girl who'd had so many plans for her horse.

Days, weeks and even months went by as I tried to work through the grief. Sometimes Christie looked so sad and when I hugged her, she would only say "I'm missing Sable." She would ask what I thought Sable was doing in heaven and if I thought she was happy there. Christie would tell me Sable was her best friend and I could understand why. Each night when I tucked her in, she would say her prayers and ask God to take care of her special little mare. "Do you still miss Sable Mommy?" she would ask me with a deep sadness in her eyes. I could only hold her and let my tears flow, as there were no words of comfort and only endless explanations.

Sable had been the only horse we had, so there was a big void in our lives now. Both of us missed the riding and horse care. We missed the contact and passion that flows in the blood of a horse lover, the pleasure and relaxation of afternoon rides, the companionship of the stable chores we had shared. After much thought, I decided to get another horse and began looking even though I knew I couldn't bring back the one we'd lost. I could only hope Christie would find the strength to work through her grief with my love and support.

I made a list of requirements for this new horse and began calling friends, stables, tack shops and breeders. I scouted magazines, billboards, newspapers, riding schools, horse shows and auctions. I wrote lots and lots of letters, pouring out my heart to complete strangers. The people at the gas station loved me, as I frequently fueled up and with Christie as my sidekick, headed off on our search. We covered a lot of territory, met wonderful people and rode a lot of super horses.

At one point, we went to a stable that had a number of horses for sale. Christie ran to the stall of a big mare from the track. She was chestnut with a blaze just like Sable and that made Christie's heart flutter. It made mine wilt. I tried not to like the mare and told myself to pick her apart objectively. When we opened the stall door, the mare lowered her head to Christie. She was unsure what to do with her, but curious and gentle, with an inquisitive eye.

While being ridden, the mare moved nicely and although green, she seemed very willing. When I got on myself, it was as refreshing as a warm spring rain. There was an immediate connection, a flow of warmth and power aching to express itself. I didn't want this mare to be in my heart, but she was already there.

When I left the barn, emotion overwhelmed me as I realized that I had made my decision. This mare was young enough to accept training but well past the coltish stage. She was good breeding and performance stock, a very strong animal; she seemed very willing and adaptable. The price was right, so I thought about it for a week and continued to look at other horses all the while. I didn't want my emotions making a decision for me, but I couldn't get that mare off my mind and it seemed neither could Christie. She mentioned a few times how soft the nose was, what a pretty face and how she could touch the sky from the mare's back.

I finally called and made an offer. After a vet confirmed that all was well, arrangements were made for delivery the following week. The new mare arrived on a Wednesday and seemed to settle in nicely. I didn't encourage a lot of contact between the new horse and Christie, because I felt that the child might still have unresolved emotions and I wanted to give her time to deal with those. She came to the barn with me frequently and played in the fields while I rode. She shed a few tears, because it was impossible to do with the new mare what she had done with Sable. I didn't push the relationship and Christie seemed content just to be around the stable.

Our mare had never been around children, especially not young active ones that did the least expected things at the least expected times. She tended to be a flighty mare and had broken her share of snaps and leads, but this little blond that was always around kind of worked on her curiosity. Christie would reach up through the bars of the stall and pat the soft nose. Her touch was gentle and kind, probably much kinder than anything the mare had experienced before. After the mare's workout, Christie would sometimes sit in the saddle and brush her, stroking the soft neck and talking to her all the while. The big chestnut never offered to move and as I stood there watching, she became more calm and relaxed, thriving on the extra attention. Christie and our new addition seemed to be in their own little world.

As the warmth of summer came, Christie seemed to blossom with her new-found friend. She would share her deepest feelings with the mare, even though she hadn't found the words with human kind. One day, she expressed concern to the new mare that Sable would feel hurt and left out if we went on without her and cared for our new horse. I couldn't let that thought linger, so I explained to my daughter that Sable had loved her and wouldn't want to see her sad. I tried to tell Christie that Sable

50

would always be in her heart. She just wasn't in a place where we could pat her or put the saddle on and go for a ride, although we still look toward the stall and expect to see her there. I told her she could remember all the fun there had been in the times they had together. Those memories would always be there to love and to cherish. If Sable and this new horse had known each other, they would probably be friends and even share the same pasture.

As if knowing what the conversation was about, the new mare nickered a bit and nuzzled Christie's arm. It was like she had a sixth sense. This mare from the track with a different owner for every year of her life had some qualities no one had found yet. Her deep brown eyes had a depth I could only feel. It was like she was saying, "Don't worry over explaining things. Just leave Christie be and let it happen." And I could trust her with my little girl's heart. That seemed my only choice and for sure the wisest.

We took the mare out to the paddock and Christie climbed the fence. Our chestnut visited for a while and then wandered away to nip some mouthfuls of sweet grass. The day was warm and bright so we just stood there leaning on the fence to soak in the sunshine for a while. The sky was clear blue with not a cloud in sight. The trees had a gentle sway, to and fro. An occasional bee landed on the pink clover blossoms and butterflies danced in the air. Our world was a peaceful, quiet place.

Christie broke the silence by saying she'd decided what to call the new mare. She had a registered name, but it was too long for everyday use, so Christie thought we should call the mare Red, because that's how she looked in the field. The way the sun shone on her that day, she was a bright, beautiful chestnut with every color of a summer sunset glistening on her coat. Christie called the name out and the mare must have approved, because she reached down, took another mouthful of grass and sauntered over to us.

I decided now was the time to tell Christie the mare was in foal. I explained that over the long winter months her tummy would grow and in the spring there would be a baby dancing in the fields. I told Christie that Red would need special attention to her diet, occasional vet visits and lots of tender love and caring. Christie wanted to know if Red would have to go to a horsey hospital for the birth. I told her no, she could probably manage that herself and we would just walk out to the barn one day and meet the new foal. Christie, of course, decided it should be a filly so she could put a pink halter on it. She also ordered a camera for Christmas so she could take pictures of the baby. She told Red not to worry. She would be in the pictures, too.

Christie asked me what we were going to name the new baby and I didn't have a clue. I know the name of a registered horse is supposed to carry on the name of their parentage, but I really hadn't given it any serious thought. It dawned on me that maybe Christie should name the baby and as we walked toward the house, I asked her if she would like to. Seeing the excitement in her eyes was answer enough, so I promised her that when the foal was born she could name it. As time passes, so do troubles of the heart. At least that is what happened here. For the past few months she has been able to talk about Sable, reminiscing about the things they did with a happy heart.

Looking at photographs of Sable as a foal, Christie remarked how sassy and cute she was. She made up her own little album for all her horsey friends; Sable, Red, a picture of the stallion Red is bred to and a few empty pages for the new foal.

Christie rushes home from school to ride Red in the paddock, practicing walk, trot and whoa. Red has become docile in her pregnant state. I think she realizes there will be two to look after, a fuzzy little foal and a tag-along kid. Christie has taken pictures of Red to school to ' Show and Tell' about pregnant mares. She has decided on a name for the foal and seems to have put a lot of thought into it. My daughter explained to me that Sable made her feel warm in her heart until she died. Then her heart felt all achy and sore. The little girl thought hurt would always be there. It would never go away. For a while she didn't want it to. She told me that as time went on, the hurting didn't happen as much, even though she still thought a lot about Sable. She said that even after the hurt went away, thinking about Sable made her feel warm inside, and even though she still misses her she knows Sable won't be back. Christie went on to tell me there is a warm place in her heart for Red, "cause when I think of her mommy, it makes me feel warm inside too. I'd love her even if she wasn't going to have a baby, but I love her more that she is. I want to name the baby Beautiful Heart, so when I think of her, my heart will be warm."

A gentle touch, a timely glance, a soft nuzzle placed on a child's sleeve. Horses have paved the way to a lifelong experience for my child.

This mare, Red, has taught Christie things I couldn't begin to explain. Her persistence made an injured little soul want to live again; not only live, but also reach for life's glory and bask in it. For a species so gentle and kind, for a mare so persistent in giving, for a long-awaited foal so inquisitive and trusting, what better name than Beautiful Heart?

Spring finally arrived and one crisp sunny morning while the dew still hung in the air, Red gave birth without a problem. Christie was still in her nightie, but with sleep in her eyes I took her out to meet the new little filly. The blond child stood for a few moments in awe. It seemed like she was still dreaming. Her big blue eyes were full of amazement with a few tears gathered in the corners. She reached out a hand and the little filly nuzzled her curiously. Christie took a few steps closer and threw her arms around the new foal's neck. They both tumbled gently into the straw and lay there contentedly, patting and nuzzling each other with care. Welled-up tears spilled onto the new baby's coat and emotion held thick to the air. Christie whispered "Beautiful Heart" as a little tear tickled her cheek. It seemed a fitting name and all was well. Red and I stood back and watched a fuzzy, still-wet foal tickle the heart of a child and the child tickled back. They giggled and snorted and touched.

How gently can a horse touch the heart of a child? Gently enough to help her forget the pain of death, to teach her that life goes on; gently enough to nudge her into friendship with innocence as the backbone of their souls; gently enough to show that love and the cycle of life are infinite and strong; gently enough to do all this without the child aware and to teach her the warmth of a beautiful heart. A little pink halter now hangs outside her best friend's stall.

Cindy Mitchell

Biography: Cindy Mitchell. "I was born and raised in the Eastern Townships of Quebec. Animals, and particularly horses, have always been my closest friends. I am married with three children - Sean, Christina and Natalie - who have been a great source of inspiration and enjoyment to me. A registered nurse by profession, I have a lifelong interest in writing poetry and prose. I ride as often as I can and am involved with local clubs as well as the Ontario Standardbred Adoption Society. As a matter of interest, Beautiful Heart is the first Appaloosa frozen semen baby in the world!"

Bordering Baby

One Sunday, as my husband and I were taking a Sunday drive to a scenic country area in the mountains one mile above our desert home, we were unexpectedly involved in a great round-up adventure.

Frequently we visit a beautiful, secluded community in the San Jacinto Mountains known as Garner Valley. It is a pristine, rural area, well known to hikers and equestrians, as part of the Pacific Crest Trail runs through it. There are mostly horse and cattle ranches of grandeur, with great expanses of pasture and treed forests. My love of horses takes me to this place whenever I need to get away from the everyday stresses of a fast-paced life in a busy desert city.

We had packed a wholesome picnic lunch, backpacks, water bottles and well-worn hiking boots. The morning was fresh and clear and sunny (as always)!

We pulled off the main road and parked in an area designated for equestrians and hikers. We spent hours hiking and exploring, and brought along a digital camera for memories and later viewing. On a ridge high above the valle/ we rested and devoured our lunch.

At this point, we were happy but tired and decided to return to our car and drive along some of the back roads before driving down the mountain to our home. We turned down a very winding, secluded country road with lovely worn, white wood fences that stretched for miles. Horses dotted the peaceful pastures and the sun shone through a tunnel of trees as we drove slowly down the lane, enjoying every minute.

Suddenly, just ahead of our car, three horses boldly ran across the road in front of us with no riders. Two were adult horses and the third was a very young colt. We quickly noticed that the pasture fence had broken and the horses were cleverly escaping. There was no one else around to get them back into their corral.

We pulled off to the opposite side of the road and got out of the car to try and herd them back to their pasture. It was somewhat amusing to see eight mares peering over the fence, watching the entire event from another property along the same road. The colt became curious and approached the onlookers. As he neared them to nuzzle, the mares all attempted to push him back, as if to be communicating to him that he should go back home where he belonged.

My husband, in the meantime, was inspecting the broken fence rail and removed the broken piece, and as he did this, the two adult horses were drawn like magnets directly back to their own pasture with no effort whatsoever on our part. My husband slid a fence rail back to secure the fence until we could round up the colt, as he had been busy prancing up and down the street, investigating everything except us. He was clearly going to be a problem to coax back into his pasture. We both made several attempts to calmly speak to him and to slowly approach him, but he was timid, frightened and extremely stubborn. His momma began calling for him from the opposite side of the pasture fence and he became frantic and decided to bolt and run down the street again and again. He always returned, knowing the other horses were calling for him. We made several more attempts to get him into the pasture, but nothing worked as we tried a small rope and a little pulling and a bit of pushing. He wanted no part of us and stood his ground very firmly.

We attempted to call the owners, as there was a sign on their ranch gate, but no one answered. We tried several more times to coax the colt back home. Nothing was working. Finally, in the distance from a long wooded driveway leading from the main ranch house, I saw three dogs running towards us. I then noticed that two of the dogs stopped and stayed near the ranch as one lone dog ran towards us. He darted through the break in the fence towards us and we both knew immediately that he was a Border Collie. He sniffed us both and wagged his tail in a fast greeting, as if to say,

I know what to do. We could see the determination and meaning in his eyes. He had work to do and he set out immediately to do it.

My husband and I were astonished at the speed and skillfulness of this medium-sized dog. He began his work at the hind hoof areas of the colt, lightly nipping at his hock area to move the colt forward toward the pasture fence. He then came around to the front of the colt and proceeded around to the back again. He was quick and repetitious in his moves. He was determined and focused. We stood near enough to the colt to guide his direction, as the Border Collie worked his magic.

The colt bolted a few times and the dog would run and round him up and lead him back. After several attempts, the colt gave in and gave a little leap and jumped right over the fence to the two adult horses awaiting him. The Border Collie followed and herded them all back to their barn and corral area. We were thrilled at seeing this natural herding event happening right before our eyes. We felt so blessed to have experienced such a memorable event, on such a perfect day up in that gorgeous mountain valley. We were also very lucky to have turned on that digital camera and have it all on film. We have both learned so much from that day in Garner Valley, where a colt and a dog naturally communicated in their own ways and through their own genuine instincts, sensed and sought safety.

Holly A. Johnson

Biography: Holly A. Johnson. Holly is an artist and animal rights activist now living in Southern California. She grew up in Rhode Island where she had her own horse and always dreamed of having a horse ranch. She now lives in an area surrounded by horses, ranches and rodeos! She is an avid painter and outdoor enthusiast. She donates her time working with horses on rescue ranches and helping with local animal care awareness events.

Good Friends

This is about my red dun grade gelding named Cody. Cody was 24 years old at the time. The stories show how different species of animals do bond.

Bo, my Weston Terrier dog, started barking wildly one night. As I turned on lights and let him outside, he bee-lined for the far pasture. I raised and showed dairy goats, which had free access to the barn. Cody and the other horses were also in this pasture. Bo was barking through the fence at a pack of dogs that were chasing my goats. As I turned on more lights, Cody was herding the goats into the barn. When all were in, he turned around so his rear was facing out. He was ready to kick any dog that tried to approach. All animals were safe and the pack left. I was amazed at the teamwork of dog, horse, and goats.

I also had an American Quarter Horse gelding named "Dream." He became close friends with one goat named "Heaven Lee," and a cat named "Katlee." There was so much trust and love between them that the three would lie down in the pasture together. My husband and I would laugh and call them the three Musketeers.

Joyce E. Rienzo

Biography: Joyce E. Rienzo. "Living in New York State, we enjoy trail riding and carriage driving in the four seasons. My husband John and my identical twin sister Janet also share this love for horses and all animals. Janet and I also enjoy showing dogs in obedience trials. John and I are involved in the restoration of DIVCO trucks. Cody was a special horse. He had an accident that left him blind in his right eye and eventually it had to be removed. Cody lived to be 29 years old. My love for animals directed me to a career as a licensed veterinary technician. I was also a veterinary technician in the US Army Reserve. I'm currently in graduate school for library science and information."

The Horse Who Ate The Judge's Hat

Our 4-H club, The Hoofbeats, hosted its annual horse show at a beautiful, high pasture on Tower Hill, with a clear view of Narragansett Bay in southern Rhode Island. That pasture lay dormant all year long, coming to life just once each June with the chaos of ponies, horses and kids – all hoping for a taste of victory.

This backdrop served as the scene of my very first horse show. At the age of seven, Goldie and I would compete in the walk-trot division. Goldie was an aged mare of unremarkable breeding, a sweet school horse bought in a two-for-one deal to get her half-Morgan filly for my older brother's 4-H project. The old mare was gentle and obedient – a good match for a young girl in her first competition.

I was dressed in canary breeches, a black hunt coat my mother sewed for me, and a black derby that had been passed down through my father's family. My curly blonde hair sprang from beneath the edges of the formal hat, an elastic chin band sewn in to keep it from springing off my head.

I started riding at the age of four and was a confident rider at seven, cantering with ease in the comfort of the pastures of Old Congdon Farm, where we boarded our horses. But at the show grounds, my confidence retreated. I was almost paralyzed with fear! I don't remember anything about my class – how I got into the ring, how I maneuvered the walk-trot commands – nothing. But what I do remember vividly was the final line-up.

The judge, Dr. MacLennon, a local vet known for his signature straw topper, called us into the center of the ring. He then made a final walk down the line while he noted his placings on his scorecard. When the old vet passed Goldie and I, Goldie slipped from her usual sleepy stance and stepped forward to investigate. One step forward, then two . . . three . . . what was she doing? I was capable of halting her, but I was too frozen with fear to do anything but sit there and watch like an indifferent bystander. Four steps forward and Goldie was standing nose-to-nose with Dr. MacLennon. Then I watched in dismay as the old mare reached a little higher with her soft muzzle and took a chomp out of the judge's straw hat! A shocked Dr. MacLennon snatched his hat back from the curious mare and the spectators at ringside dissolved into laughter.

The old derby sits on my bedroom shelf to this day, covered with more dust than I should publicly admit. But when I see it, I can't help but chuckle at this memory – one of many fabulous memories of a life filled with horses.

Suzann E. Johnson

Biography: Suzann E. Johnson. Suzann started riding in earnest at the age of four, but skipped the pony stage, preferring instead the family horse, 16.2-hand Mr. Dillon. Growing up in Wakefield, Rhode Island, she was very involved in 4-H horse activities, which garnered numerous honors and awards. Suzann took a brief hiatus from horses to earn a B.S. in Foods and Nutrition and a M.S. in Nutrition and Communications. She now lives on Frog's Leap Farm in White House Station, New Jersey, with her husband Art and the world's most beautiful Golden Retriever, Tucket. Her antidote to her job in the pharmaceutical industry is her Hannoverian-Thoroughbred cross, Zydeco. Suzann also enjoys ice skating, traveling, and hunting for antiques for her 18th-century home.

Chapter Four
Overcoming Adversity

A Quest For Symmetry:
A Freak Accident Becomes A New Opportunity

I believe that *what* you think has a great effect on the outcome of an event. The event, in this instance, was my riding accident, and the outcome is my continuing recovery from a TBI (traumatic brain injury).

What actually happened was in the left lead canter of a flat class, Nicole (my young mare) lost her footing behind and went down under me and got right back up, leaving me on the ground unconscious. Although I have no memory of approximately five minutes prior until the 4th or 5th day in the Rehabilitation Hospital (about two weeks), what they called progressive amnesia, I did see a video of the accident taken by someone taping another competitor in the same class.

Although there are hundreds of thousands of mild TBI's sustained in this country every year, my TBI was more severe than most, and was therefore labeled "moderate." The specific medical name for my injury was a Coup Contre' Coup which translates to "blow by blow". It describes an injury in which the brain hits the skull on one side and then bounces over and hits the other side of the skull. At the time it happened, I was instantly rendered unconscious, and then suffered two weeks of post-traumatic amnesia. It took five months before I felt ready to send for my medical records, and began asking the questions I now wanted the answers to.

What I learned was that I was unconscious longer than six hours (6 hours or longer indicates a more severe TBI) and was in a semi-comatose state. I also learned that my correctly fitting helmet with chinstrap was removed in the emergency room. I was in the ICU for four days, and my family was told that I was "a very pleasant patient."

The neurosurgeon who first examined me thought at first that I would recover in a few days. When it became apparent that this was not the case, I was moved to the brain injury floor of a rehabilitation hospital. It was there that I "woke up". It was a very gradual and "foggy" awakening. For two weeks I had a taste of the reality of life as a paraplegic. I was only able to get around in a wheelchair pushed by a nurse, and was transported for tests at other facilities in a wheelchair van. With daily physical, speech and occupational therapy sessions, I slowly progressed from wheelchair to walker. When I asked to go home (at the earliest opportunity) I used a walker for a month while I practiced with my new cane.

At home, tasks as basic as getting up and down stairs, using the toilet and bathing were a major challenge every day. Emotionally, I was filled with gratitude for my fiancé, Ray, and for my students and friends who kept the barn going and the horses cared for while I recovered. The physical result of my head injury was ataxia, resulting in a partial paralysis of my right side from hip to toe. I felt that I was dragging a concrete block with my right hip. This basically left me with no balance at all.

Although, looking back, I was a prime candidate for a serious depression and the medication prescribed for it, there were two things I think prevented it for me. First, I had no regrets about what I did, and I had a life I very much wanted to get back to. A life that demanded a lot of time and effort, and it also required me to be physically active and shoulder a great deal of responsibility. I knew I had many "levels" of recovery to go through to get back to that life.

Today, 13 months following my accident, I can rate myself at level eight, with ten being the highest level possible. Once it was hard to even try to answer the question "How are you?" Now I answer with enthusiasm "I'm glad to be here and it's great to have the first year behind me." I know from others that it can take five to ten years for a full recovery. I'm shooting for a recovery at 110%. If I only shoot for 100%, I might fall short. I've found a bolder voice to inspire others and my students, and I'm enjoying it immensely.

My riding rehab is progressing slowly and steadily, and I could write a book on riding the walk! I compare my progress to that of a turtle, slow and strong, but it gets there. I'm still going to special physical therapy. I still have a long way to go, but now I have even more reasons for my recovery. This injury has forced me to work on my asymmetry from scoliosis, with a longer, weak left side and shorter, strong right side, something I dealt with before my injury, but had no time to change.

My right leg was affected most by the brain injury and will come back with a lot of rehabilitation. I have great therapists. They say I'm doing very well. Certain qualities come to mind, which are definite requirements to achieve a successful rehabilitation after an injury like mine; courage, patience and determination, which are also the requirements for success with horses. So the way I see it, I'm up for the task.

Lani Wicks

Biography: Lani Wicks. Lani teaches, trains and consults from Fairhaven Farm in Gonic (Rochester), New Hampshire. Her focus is on classical riding with the comfort and willingness of the horse, and the safety, confidence and understanding of the rider. Having ridden well over 100 horses of many different breeds, and held positions as groom/rider, farm/stable manager, show groom, to trainer, competitor, instructor, she has been full time since May 1982. Lani has experienced the sporthorse disciplines of Dressage, Combined Training,

Showhunters O/F, U/S, in hand, Foxhunting, distance pleasure and competitive rides. She has bred and trained two sporthorses from her mare to keep. She utilizes Bodywork with Groundwork to find pain and solve problems in the horse. Lani travels within 40 miles to work with clients. You can speak with Lani directly at Fairhaven Farm, 80 Church Street, Gonic, New Hampshire 03839-5200 or by phone at 603-335-5256.

Stop Looking For Zebras

A childhood dream, a yearning. The aching of a horse-crazed child; a longing and an emptiness that could never be fulfilled. After many twists and turns throughout my life, I felt it was time for *me*. Time for *my* needs. I made the decision: now was the time to get that horse I never had.

After taking a few riding lessons, I knew this was the missing link in my life. So on April 9, 1998, I went to look at a horse on consignment. Being a green rider and knowing nothing of the horse world, I trusted the people who were giving me the lessons and knew the seller. After all, a green rider knows little of conformation, training, vices, etc. The steed in question was a gelding, which was what I wanted, but he was a red dun. He had a white star, stripe, and a snip on his face and he even had a racing stripe down his back. But I really wanted a black or black-and-white horse - yuck, red! I was so excited, though, and of course, I was only going to look. The horse was young, just turned four, and he apparently only needed work on his lope.

There are some old sayings such as, "never judge a book by its cover" and "a good horse is never a bad color." Well, he seemed really quiet and liked to be touched. He nudged me to pet him, so I took him.

The deal was that if he didn't work out for me, their friends would take him off my hands. I should have seen the signs right then and there. They had a business practice of selling horses to inexperienced people so you would spend all that money on the horse and training, then they would take them off your hands. How thoughtful! So this green rider got a green horse, and they saw green dollar signs.

Training started for my Dundee and the lessons seemed to become fewer and farther between. A month later, I had a fall and it set my confidence back. It took me a long time to get over how much you hurt all over from a fall, especially at my age. After two months, the lessons always seemed to be over before I got there. They would say, "I just finished working him," or, "Oh, you just missed the lesson." Well, more flags started to wave and in my heart I knew something wasn't quite right.

By mid-summer, I rode only occasionally, mostly with help from other boarders. The trainer was too busy and lessons had basically stopped. During our first summer,

I mainly took Dundee out for walks and to eat grass and we rode at the walk and trot. By October, Dun started having difficulty urinating, so I had their vet check him. Another big mistake, and he did not improve throughout December either.

By mid-January 1999, Dun became worse. He had a severe attack and collapsed on the ground, gasping for air. I heard, "I'll buy him from you!" The final warning, my horse was dying and they wanted to buy him! A friend took us to an equine hospital for testing and Dundee was diagnosed with a bladder infection with crystallization.

Over the next few weeks, he had two more mild attacks. I had Dundee's mane hair DNA tested at the University of California Davis School of Veterinary Medicine and it came back positive for HYPP, N/H. My horse had a life-threatening genetic gene, Hyperkalemic Periodic Paralysis, a bladder infection, and was being stressed by cruel training techniques. He was being spurred, whipped, and they used severe bits – and God only knows what else. They also fed him straight alfalfa during the winter months with no turnout.

I had another vet evaluate him and made the decision to move him to another barn to convalesce. I did not trust this place, these people. I was a wreck and my horse was a wreck. Still, I felt this horse was good; he just needed the right road to trot down. However, what was I going to do with an unfinished horse I could barely ride? I knew nothing about training horses.

Before February ended, I moved on to another stable for a few months of rest and relaxation, and to look for a good trainer. I had Jan M. Thomas of Glory-Be Stables evaluate Dundee. Jan is a godsend to the horse world. She uses gentle techniques, and has the knack to 'talk to the animals.' Yes, she is a Dr. Dolittle. She did whispering long before it became famous. I knew in my heart this was the person I wanted to finish him. Heck, he only needed work on his lope. Surely after eight months of training at the other place he should have been almost finished by now! Well, Dundee knew nothing: no leg commands, no neck reining, and he could barely back up. Jan did not have much hope for him, as Dundee was afraid to trust her. He wanted to trust, but he had so much baggage to carry it was nearly impossible. I was devastated.

In my heart and soul, I knew this misguided horse was good. Why would God make me wait 42 years for a horse and he not be the one for me? I believe in fate and this was our destiny.

During our third year, we struggled and worked extremely hard, and we are doing well, even though I had three nasty falls and officially got my pilot's license for "flying". I also wrecked my finger, had a concussion, got two huge bruises on my bottom, knocked my hips out of joint twice, had the wind knocked out of me, and cracked my Mickey Mouse limited edition helmet. I bought two saddles – one new one, because Dundee needed full quarter horse bars – paid for training (twice over), and spent a hefty amount on equine medical bills. I also bought a used horse trailer and paid to fix Jan's saddle (the one that Mel Gibson once sat on) because Dun wrecked it in his first two weeks of training. We went through two farriers and two vets until I found good ones. All this in less than three years – should I go on? But I still love the horse world.

Today, we are riding in a bosal because Dun's mouth was ruined. Dundee now has trust, a good home, and much love and compassion. He is excellent on the trail, is solid – a tank – and has a trot to die for. Even though Dun is such a bratty horse, he still makes my life so bearable. He takes away all the pain and stresses of life and makes each day worth living. Dun is that void I could never fill; an expensive void, mind you, but he makes me so very happy.

When I look at Dun, I smile. We are soul mates; one mate that has no words, but speaks with flowing, graceful movements, and one that is ecstatic that the good Lord above has given him to me to take care of and love. Although I tend to look for I know not what, Jan always tells me to "stop looking for zebras!"

I will never forget the first few times in the round pen at Glory-Be Stables, watching Dundee's equine body language and talking to this beautiful creature on his terms. My eyes still well with tears whenever I think of that first join-up, when he came to me with trust, with love, and he accepted our new life together. A life with no pain, no stress, just mutual respect – most days. We still have much to learn, however, but we have survived. My heart just could not give up on him after knowing of his past life. I know our fourth year will be even better with trail rides, possibly a horse show, and the rest of our lives together as horse and rider.

There is nothing more beautiful than when I enter into the barn and Dundee whinnies to me. Sometimes it is my voice he hears; sometimes it is just my presence. Whatever it is, it is surely magical and these few precious seconds make all the world a more wonderful place to be.

Oh, did I mention? He is a beautiful red dun - and I would not trade him for any black or black-and-white horse in the world.

JoAnn M. Silva

Biography: JoAnn M. Silva. JoAnn lives near Nazareth, Pennsylvania, with her husband, mother, a twice-rescued Jack Russell Terrier, and two cats. Dundee, her horse, boards at Glory-Be Stables in Stroudsburg. Being a horse-crazy child that never recovered, she purchased her first equine mate at age 42. The horse world filled a huge void where equine blood flows through her veins and takes her breath away. JoAnn's writing credits consist of a horse journal, many poems, some children's stories, and many ideas for paper and ink when time permits.

A Therapy Horse For All Seasons Of The Heart

When the stars line up just right, something wonderful happens. It began when Robert and Portia Sue Owens of Moondance Ranch accepted a one-week-old miniature horse in trade for training a horse for a client's granddaughter. For a brief moment, the allure of entering a young miniature horse stallion in the competitive world of national horse shows beckoned strongly. As a yearling, Cheyenne was fitted with a bit and taken to a spring show in Boring, Oregon, and later to one in Monroe, Washington. Cheyenne was sold to a Washington couple for their herd sire with a money-back guarantee if his second testicle failed to drop by the time he turned three.

Tragedy struck in 1996. Extensive surgery for the undescended testicle ended Cheyenne's show career and usefulness as a stud. Robert and Portia make a living by filling their stalls with training horses, and were feeling a bit desperate when fate stepped in.

In a small town in Idaho, volunteers, staff and residents involved with the WTRRA Equine Experiences for the Elderly Program were frustrated. At the time, people were driven from the Discovery Care Center in a van to the local fairgrounds. They were unable to transport all those who wanted to participate, plus many could not travel due to their fragile health. In an attempt to meet these needs, staff took adult horses to the care center. This still meant moving people to visit the horses outside and if the weather was bad, their equine experience was canceled.

"Why not get a miniature horse?" someone asked. "We can take it inside the care center." A guiding star led them to the Moondance Ranch in Oregon. As Portia wrote, "A few e-mails, a handy transport and off he went to the Whitewater Therapeutic Riding and Recreation Association. My worst-money horse deal turned into the best-heart horse deal."

Cheyenne, renamed Tater Tots, exemplifies the role of a therapy horse not only for the elderly, but also for the youth in our community. Although tiny in stature, his huge heart embodies the spirit of our therapy programs. He has opened the world of horses for ages two to 92.

By first introducing children to Tater Tot, who is nearer their height than a regular horse, we eliminate their initial fear of size. This process also works with adults who are hesitant to approach the larger-size animal. This method makes for a smoother transition to our therapy program, where the individual is mounted on a full-size horse.

At the Discovery Care Center each week, Tater Tot initiates both emotional and physical participation from the elderly and the staff. Memory lines to the past are established as the elderly revive and relive their associations with horses. Tater Tot senses and responds to their individual needs for nurturing. When he approaches a person, he places his head on their lap or stomach. His eyes close. Peace embraces horse and human. Tater Tot continues to amaze us with his timely departure from each individual. For some it's a short and gentle greeting, while with others he lingers.

Some of the residents delight in practicing an old or new skill — driving. Settled in Tater Tot's cart, they ask and he responds by pulling them down the hallways of the care center. For some, it's an outing with a horse and cart, driving in downtown Salmon. Others desire his company from their sitting chair or the bedside; a time to talk of earlier years while he listens with an open heart. Moments of tenderness are found as he nuzzles a hand that reaches for his unconditional love. Hearts find a new melody and souls breathe harmony.

On some star-studded night, I'm sure Tater Tot heard a whisper on the wind… *As a shining star in Salmon, Idaho, you are fulfilling your destiny as a therapy horse for all seasons of the heart.*

Margaret C. Hevel

Biography: Margaret C. Hevel. "I was a consultant and reviewer for educational materials with Marsh Film Co., Kendall School for the Deaf, WA. D.C. and Gallaudet College. As a Nurse Health Educator, I was founder and director of a child abuse/neglect prevention program. I presented at workshops, seminars and conferences in the northwest and nationally. My poems and short stories have been published in magazines and newspapers. I have written four novels. The last one was in collaboration with my daughter and I am a driving instructor with the WTRRA Equine Therapeutic Program."

The Long And Winding Road

I first met Mickie when she was three. At the time, I had no idea she would be gracing the pasture at our farm. My cousin's husband, Billy, was training a few racehorses and had invited me to visit him at a local racetrack. Mickie was a pretty filly, a dark roan. Several weeks later, I noticed her name on the racing schedule in the newspaper, so I went to the track and bet two dollars on her. She finished dead last.

All I ever wanted was a horse. My parents sent me to riding lessons and summer camps. They briefly leased a horse for me, but couldn't afford to buy and keep one. I offered to give up or do anything to get one, but to no avail. I was determined that when I grew up, I was going to live on a farm and have my own perfect dream horse just like Black Beauty – or even better, several horses.

The years passed. I went away to college where I met my future husband, Dan. After graduation, we moved back to New Hampshire. We got engaged and went looking for a farm. We purchased a small house on a few acres with a barn. The walls and stall partitions inside the barn were made of two-by-10 inch rough-cut oak. Beautiful! The only thing missing was the horse.

When I started horse shopping, I gave Billy a call to ask if he would help. Instead, he offered to give me Mickie in exchange for taking care of his gelding for the winter. Mickie was four at the time and had finally won a race, but being a racehorse was not for her. Billy thought it best that she retire from racing while she was still sound and could learn a new trade. Happily, Mickie came to our farm in the fall of 1991.

I let her relax for a month. The first time I tried to ride her, I didn't even get a leg over her back. She dumped me in the dirt, took off and broke her bridle. It was the first in a succession of similar events. She would only tolerate me on her back if we were led around the corral.

However, by the spring of 1992, Mickie and I were walking and trotting on our own. I was just beginning to trust her when, with Dan and my father watching, she bolted through the barn. I was anticipating a quick stop and subsequent launch into a fence right behind the barn door, when something hit the top of my head, forcing me down and back – hard – into the saddle. It was the top of the oak door frame. Mickie stopped and I landed on the fence. At first, I thought I was dead. I reached up, fully expecting not to find my head. Later, I noticed that my head had cracked the oak door frame.

Fortunately, I didn't break any bones, but had severely strained both my neck and upper back, tearing the muscles attached to my left shoulder blade. The doctor informed me that I could have been paralyzed or dead, which, he thought, was the better option. I could hardly move for months. Secretly, I was glad to have an excuse not to ride. The worst injury was to my "nerve."

Summer and fall passed. Then, one morning in January, I went out to the barn to find that Mickie hadn't eaten the breakfast Dan had left out earlier. Entering her stall, I found her left hind leg bloody and swollen. When our vet arrived, he discovered that

Mickie had peeled the skin from her leg, exposing about eight inches of her cannon bone. Dr. Fallon stitched her back together, bandaged her up, and left instructions for medication, cleaning and bandaging the wound. He said it would be a long road back, but believed the tendons and bone were undamaged. If we were lucky, she might avoid skin grafts. For the next six months, I cleaned, treated and bandaged that leg. Finally, Dr. Fallon pronounced her healed and ready for work.

We began taking walks. Barely a month had passed when Mickie became lame in both front feet. Dr. Fallon examined her and found symptoms of navicular syndrome. I thought this was the beginning of the end, but he was hopeful. Mickie began a course of medication and special shoeing. Just as there were signs of improvement, Dr Fallon had to come back again, this time for an eye injury. Then it was my turn; Mickie reached over to grab a mouthful of hay out of my arms and hit my head with hers. This resulted in five stitches to my eyebrow and a hole in my cornea. It was quite painful and I was seeing double for weeks.

Two months later, Mickie bolted into the barn, crashed into a stall door and opened her shoulder. Dr. Fallon came out to put "Humpty Dumpty," back together again. It was suggested at this point that I might consider finding a different home for Mickie. I have to admit I gave it some thought. These accidents weren't helping my confidence. There was something about her, though, and I hadn't run out of options or hope.

It took all my courage to get on her again. True to form, she bucked and bolted. I became an emergency dismount expert, but the bruises took their toll on my mind and body. In the fall, I hired a girl to ride her. She did manage to stay on. In the spring, I began again, only to be promptly dumped while my husband watched. Dan had a talk with me. He didn't want to be a widower and couldn't fathom all the time and money wasted on something I couldn't enjoy. He suggested I make a decision about my horse, one way or another.

I told my friend, Jan, my dilemma. Her daughter had started taking riding lessons at a new farm and she thought the people there might be helpful. Jan introduced me to Kim and Warren Meyer. They were hopeful and agreed to take Mickie for training in August. Kim and Warren's philosophy is, as Kim put it, "holistic." They took Mickie back to square one, treating her like a foal just learning to put a halter on. They found a way to communicate with her and began to find the holes in her training. They also re-educated me.

I began taking riding lessons with Kim on their horses to improve my ability and confidence. Piece by piece, we put it back together: groundwork, round pen work, free lunging, lunging and finally, by the fall of 1997, I was riding Mickie. A year later, while I was five months pregnant, we did our first hunter pace/trail ride.

We recently attended our first clinic together. The clinician commented to my father about the remarkable bond between my horse and I. It is amazing where you can go when you have a little hope and you don't give up.

Mary R. Wall

Biography: Mary R. Wall. Mary and Mickie are currently living on a small farm in southern New Hampshire. They share the farm with Mary's husband and little boy, a chubby pony, three happy dogs and seven chickens. They continue to train and improve with the Meyers. Mickie has changed from a dark roan to a light dapple gray. Mary has a few more gray hairs herself. "My riding background has always been predominantly English, but we hope to begin working cows and perhaps do some team penning one day."

My Boy Bill

My chestnut grade horse, Bill, is what's known as a character. Of all the horses we've owned, he's definitely my favorite. As for memories of him, who could possibly forget?

Who could forget the time my daughter was eventing him, and we walked the course the day before and viewed a wide, coffin-shaped jump filled with apples.

"Bill isn't going to jump food," I said matter-of-factly.

My daughter asked for a dime and threw it into one of two wishing wells which formed the side of another large jump. "I wish," she said, "to live."

Bill started around the course the next day with no great enthusiasm. Still, he doggedly negotiated each obstacle. Then he came to the apples.

It *looked* like Bill was going to jump. He was actually in jumping position when his nostrils quivered and he took a sudden turn to the right. Then he came around again and stopped dead, straining to get at the apples.

"He's afraid of the jump," said one of the officials helpfully. He then took an apple and showed it to Bill to let him see there was nothing in the coffin to be afraid of. At the next approach, Bill not only veered to the right, he also managed to grab an apple and gallop around with pieces of it spewing from his mouth.

68

At that point, the officials gave up and actually removed a top plank from a neighboring fence. Bill was allowed to jump the fence instead of the apples, effectively eliminating him. He finished the course, taking the last and biggest jump with great style. By then, he had been passed by the horse coming behind, whose starting time was eight minutes after his!

Memories of Bill were captured time and again by our local newspaper;

Bill going through the Tim Horton's drive-through.
Bill in the musical ride at Summerfest six years in a row.
Bill visiting the seniors' homes.
Bill in many Santa Claus parades.
Bill in the Ride for Canada.
Bill giving rides to nursery school children.
Bill in the local "Hoof and Woof" shows.

At the "Hoof and Woof" shows, Bill was always in the horse/dog relays – one year as the dog! The audience loved it when he came onto the field with floppy spaniel ears and a scarf, and jumped riderless around a course of cavallettis.

In the fields at home, Bill is the boss of all the other horses. With adults he can often be a pest, removing hats and waving them in the air, nudging sidewalkers into puddles, licking camera lenses when people try to photograph him.

In our volunteer therapeutic riding program, however, we see another Bill. With the challenged children, Bill steps smoothly and cautiously. On an Easter Seals telethon video, you can see him standing stock still while a little boy on crutches heads unsteadily towards him. That same little boy said his first words on Bill's back.

My favorite horse? Definitely, *My Boy Bill.*

Colleen Rutherford Archer

Biography: Colleen Rutherford Archer. Colleen and her husband Andrew own a small stable in Deep River, Ontario, where for the past 10 years Colleen and friends have run a volunteer summer riding program for challenged children. Colleen is a writer who has published over 400 articles and short stories, plus three books. "Riding High", a young adult novel about horses, is available from Penumbra Press, and "The Horse Dealer" is available from Borealis Press. "The Touch of Something Wild", another young adult novel about horses, will soon be released by Penumbra Press. Colleen has two daughters, Elizabeth and Heather, and a granddaughter, Bridget.

The Win That Almost Was

I was a young horse-crazy girl - you know the type. My dream was to have a horse that I could compete with in horse shows. I was lucky enough to have a horse-crazy dad, but his dream was to have a horse with which he could play polo.

When I turned 11 years old, he said *"we"* could start looking for that "dream" horse – but it had to be a Thoroughbred. I looked in the paper every week and found an ad for a four-year-old mare who was half Thoroughbred, half Quarter Horse.

"Can we look at this one, please?" I begged and he said, "Okay". So we made an appointment for that Saturday. I couldn't wait. One look at her in the stall and we were both hooked – she was beautiful!

"Well," Dad said, "if she rides as good as she looks, we may have our horse."

We saddled her up and Dad rode her first, announcing, "She will be perfect for polo!" Oh well, at least I have a horse to love. We took her to the stable and he started to train her and she took to it right away. We took her to a few games and she loved it. Well, I thought, "There goes my show horse."

Dad finally said I could start to ride her and she was wonderful to ride, but not my idea of a dream horse for English Pleasure classes. I was pretty bummed, but I kept riding her and one day someone suggested, "Why don't you teach her to barrel race?" After all, she was very handy and fast. So I set up some barrels and she loved it. I went to dad and told him what I had been doing and asked if we could we take her to a show in the spring.

"We'll see how well you do taking care of her and riding her," he said. Of course, he had just found himself an exercise girl.

I set up some poles and we practiced pole bending in addition to barrels. Spring came and the first show was upon us. I was so nervous and excited at the same time. We went into the first class, barrel racing, and we placed! So we went into the pole bending class and placed in it also. I was hooked. Dad said we did so well we could go into another show (if it didn't interfere with any polo games).

At our next show, I decided to add a class, so we started practicing for the keyhole race. You just run around the ring and you have to stop and stand in a large keyhole made of chalk – piece of cake.

The next show came and we moved up a few places in barrels and poles and did well in the keyhole, too. This was so much fun. We did well that entire summer and the last show was upon us. I knew I had to get a really good time to win the keyhole race. I thought if I had a pair of spurs I could get an extra edge, so I borrowed a pair and we were ready to kick some you know what!

"Ok girl, here we go," I urged. She shot off the line like a race horse and *flew* around the ring like the wind. Speed alone wasn't enough in keyhole; you had to be able to stop in the designated area. I had to stop her, so I pulled on the reins as hard as I could and she stopped in the keyhole with a bounce so hard she launched me right off.

There I was on the ground with her looking down at me. Her inquisitive look said it all, "What are you doing down there?" I was so embarrassed. I brushed myself off, looked around and yes, we were in the keyhole. I had a little laugh and we walked out of the ring. Would you believe we had the best time and we would have won – except you have to be on the horse to win. I guess I will just chalk this one up to an unforgettable experience, a lesson learned for the future – *she does not need spurs!*

That mare definitely lived up to her name "Windy". We had her until she was in her 20's. She was all heart, whether on the polo field or in the show ring – one of those *one of a kind* horses that only come into your life once in a lifetime.

Colleen Weidner

Biography: Colleen Weidner. "I live in Illinois on our "dream farmette" with my husband of 34 years. I am very grateful for his support of this passion of mine and later, of our daughter's. Our children are grown now. Our son and his wife blessed us this past spring with our first grandson. Our daughter is in college now. We shared many fun years "horsing around" at shows. I still enjoy local shows and quiet trail rides; my "gaming days" are long gone. I work at our local saddle shop and enjoy helping other horse-crazy people. My father is still playing polo at 72 years old, much to my mother's chagrin. This past summer I was lucky enough to have another girlhood dream come true. We bred my daughter's retired show mare (half Arabian/palomino) and we were blessed again with a beautiful black filly that my husband is spoiling rotten. I am enjoying looking out the window and watching her play. Life is good when you follow those dreams."

Chapter Five
A Love So Strong

Fries Anyone?

It was summertime when I first learned to ride a horse. I must have been 13 or 14 years old, and my parents had taken us to the Poconos for a vacation. One day, my stepsister, Anne, suggested we go horseback riding. Since the only real experience we'd had with horses were the pony rides at the county fair, my parents thought it best we take a lesson or two first.

It was warm that day and very dry, with barely a whisper of wind in the air. Sweat ran from under my hunt cap and into my eyes, mixing with the dust rising from the ring as my horse's hooves made contact with the dirt. I did my best to follow the instructor's commands: "Back straight, sit up tall, girls. Remember to keep those heels down! Relax, don't be so stiff. Just follow the movement of your horse."

I soon realized that riding a horse was a lot of work, both mentally and physically. And it was frustrating, too. When my heels were down, my back would slouch. If I corrected my posture, my heels came up. Up to this point, I thought riding a horse meant getting up on its back and saying, "giddy up!" Success was determined by whether you stayed on or not. That first lesson set me straight and turned me onto horses for life.

When we returned home, Anne and I started working at Willow Tree Farm. It was a small stable housing privately-owned horses and a few school horses. Our parents wanted us to experience the flip side to horseback riding and made arrangements for us to work at the farm after school and on weekends. We'd clean stalls, scrub and fill water buckets, and feed the horses in exchange for weekly riding lessons. It was tiring work, but satisfying. At the end of the day I'd get in the car to go home, exhausted and reeking of horse manure, but extremely happy and content.

The horsey seed had been planted. The next logical step? Start begging your parents for a horse of your own. Anne did most of the begging. She was much more vocal than I was, and had more influence over the primary breadwinner/decision maker in the house – her father. He'd already consented to a cat, much to my allergic mother's dismay, so why not an animal just a tad bigger?

Like every other kid that wants a pet, Anne and I promised to share it, take care of it, love it, and never, *ever* ask our parents for another thing as long as we lived. They couldn't pass up a deal like that, so they agreed. Not long after, Sunny came into our lives.

His show name was Hillcrest Cimmaron. His owner called him Hilly. He had quite a career in the show ring, advancing all the way to Maclay Medal division at the National Horse Show. Fortunately for us, Hilly's owner had outgrown him. She got as far as she could on him and needed a more versatile mount if she was to excel in the show ring. Her loss was definitely our gain.

Hilly was in his stall when I came to see him that first day. The fading afternoon light cast shadows in the barn and it was difficult to see him standing in the far corner of the stall. I opened the door and walked slowly toward him with my hand out so he could get a whiff of me. He was timid at first, but curiosity got the better of him and he stretched his neck toward my hand. The legs soon followed and he came into the light.

He stood about 16.2 hands and was a beautiful copper-colored chestnut. His coat shone like a brand new penny. His physique was a tribute to his Quarter Horse lineage and the care he'd receive from his previous owner. I felt little fear as he sniffed my hand, rubbing his nose against it and then tasting it with his tongue. Usually, I was more cautious with a horse I didn't know, but I sensed that this horse was different. I could trust him.

We decided to call him Sunny; I don't remember why. Perhaps it was the color of his coat or his cheerful disposition. I can't recall, but the name suited him. As soon as I got to the barn each day, I'd run to his stall to let him know I was there. He'd stop whatever he was doing and greet me with a snort and a gentle nudge with his soft, warm nose.

When stalls were done and horses were fed, I'd often open the door to Sunny's stall and just sit there, watching him. The smell of his hide and the sounds he made were very peaceful to me. Every now and then, Sunny would come over and nuzzle against my shoulder as if to reassure me that he enjoyed my company. I felt humbled and privileged that such a great creature would willingly allow me to be in his presence.

Saturdays were busy days at the farm. In addition to horsekeeping chores, there were lessons to take. Over the years, my stepfather's tendency towards being a perfectionist had rubbed off on me and proved to be detrimental to my riding. Trying so hard to be "perfect" when I rode caused me to become easily frustrated. I sometimes took this out on Sunny, although it was never his fault. I confused him by giving him mixed signals or I'd pull too hard on his mouth. He never retaliated, although he had every right to. He just stood there, calmly waiting for me to realize my mistakes and try again.

Saturday afternoons, all the girls at the barn would walk to the nearby deli and buy lunch, which usually consisted of some kind of chips, soda and a dessert. Anne and I would often bring Sunny back his favorite treat – French fries and pineapple soda. Certainly not the food of choice for his stomach designed for digesting hay, grain, and the occasional sugar cube, but we only indulged him now and then, so what could it hurt?

Before the fries were even out of the bag, Sunny would initiate his own style of begging by bowing his head to the inside of an out stretched front leg. He would do this repeatedly until his request was granted. Anne tried to teach him how to drink soda from the bottle, but he never quite mastered it. He had more success lapping it out of his feed tub. He was quite a sight, with catsup on his lips and pineapple soda dripping from his nose.

In the years Sunny and I were together, he gave me so much. He taught me how to be a better rider with his patience and tolerance. He made me feel needed and loved every time he nudged me or buried his nose in my hair. And he instilled in me a love for horses that has never faded over the 20-some years since I last saw him. Someday, I hope to have another horse in my life. He or she will have a tough act to follow.

Meganne K. Skerchak

Biography: Meganne K. Skerchak. Meg resides in Nazareth, Pennsylvania, with her husband and two young children. They also share their home with two golden retrievers named Jessie and Chance. College, marriage and raising a family have left little time for horses over the years, but Meg has been able to satisfy her passion by working part-time at a stable and occasionally taking riding lessons. She also had the unique opportunity of working as a volunteer foal sitter at the Mid-Atlantic Equine Medical Center in Ringoes, New Jersey. When her children are grown, and time and finances are a little freer, Meg hopes to have a horse of her own again.

A Matter Of Trust

The very first horse experience I can remember occurred at the age of five. We had six acres in the country and my parents had bought us a pony and had given a home to a retired parade horse named Coco. I would accompany my mom to the paddock at feeding time and stand next to her as both horse and pony would scurry for position at the feed buckets, but I was never scared. I was awed by horses and Coco's 17-hand palomino size never really daunted me. My first trust was in my mother. How gentle and caring she was in all aspects of her life, especially with all animals.

My sisters and I were all "horse-crazy kids" and must have driven my mom insane, because all we could talk about was riding and "playing" horse.

My father had four daughters, all blond and blue-eyed like my mom. I was born with dark hair and I was the image of my father. A horse racing fan and advanced equestrian, my dad understood me the best. At 40 years old, I can still remember him lifting me up onto that big parade horse in front of my brother. It never occurred to me to be scared. The fact there was no saddle, the size of the horse, or what could happen never crossed my mind. I picked up the reins as if I was born holding them and automatically asked Coco to walk. To this day I remember my dad's big hands on my little five-year-old waist, raising me up onto that big horse. How good it felt and I now know it was all a matter of trust.

Years have passed and both my parents are gone, but trust has lived on in my heart. It's the key to every aspect in your life and the only way I know to train horses. I have a natural instinct with horses. I am not a certified riding instructor or fancy show gal. Instead, my specialty is retraining "problem" horses and remedials. The AHSA didn't have a category for my particular trade, so finally I am listed by name. I really confused them! My understanding and work techniques have brought me to many unusual places and levels of horses, but to this day, I credit my dad and Mom for teaching me it is okay to trust. Trust has been the one thing to which I contribute my success in this field. Horses respond and work on cues, but horses excel on trust.

It would be hard to name all the horses that I have known, but among them there have been a few really special animals. One in particular was Mickey Gilley, a four-year-old Standardbred pacer I adopted. Well, supposedly Mickey was saddle broken and trail ridden, according to the agency. It turned out this wasn't really the case. Actually – not the case at all!

I found out Mickey had no ground manners, no saddle experience, but a devastatingly charming personality. This horse loved people. His way of going was big and clumsy. With his curiosity level and darling appearance, people also naturally took to Mickey, until they saw me start training him. I saddled him up for the first time and with the help of a strong farm hand holding his head I chose a large enclosed paddock to learn in. I usually prefer a round pen, but none was available on this farm. After that, nobody asked for rides on Mickey!

As soon as I reached the saddle, I felt the rocket beneath me fire up. Like a rodeo rider, I held the horn and reins and nodded to the farmhand to release us. Instinct told me what to expect and a lot of my communication skills with horses are relying on my instincts, as well as understanding theirs. Not coming off a bucking four-year-old was another thing! This bucking was our routine for the first 10 or 15 minutes of each lesson. After about five minutes I would lock my legs up high on his shoulders and with one hand, rub his neck and talk soothingly that it was okay, I understood. And after a week of this I had won him over. He trusted me. I never let him buck me off, though. That is important, so a horse learns there is no quarrel with me on his back. A more timid rider would have lost his seat and the horse would have learned how to rid himself of a rider.

The bucking stopped. Mickey Gilley learned extremely fast and he trusted me with his life. People began wondering if he was really a horse, calling him my shadow and laughing at how he followed me everywhere like a puppy dog. I loved Mickey and was sure he was mine forever.

This was not to be the case, however; because of a very violent divorce, I was forced to move Mickey twice, finally ending up at a Quarter Horse farm while I resolved my personal problems. I knew my ex couldn't get to him as he threatened and having nowhere to go for my own safety one night, I took a Navajo blanket and lay down right next to my sleeping horse and cried myself to sleep. Because I couldn't afford his board anymore, I was forced to put Mickey back into the adoption program. I met the woman who was to take him and I gave my approval.

It was one of the hardest days of my life when I loaded him onto her trailer, but I explained to him why and apologized, asking him to love and be good for someone else. He was six now and had to have a new mommy.

About a week later, I got a call from the woman saying he had bit her and kicked at her when she tried to lunge him and she didn't know what to do. My heart sank. Mickey didn't want to accept her. The one person he trusted wasn't there and he didn't want to work for her. She called a professional trainer. She called me every other day in frustration. This time he broke the cross ties and ran away. Then he stepped on her and kicked at her when she tried to groom him. I offered to go up to her farm and help her, but her husband said no. I got very little sleep worrying about Mickey. Did I do the right thing? Mickey never was a biter. Other than his first bucking sprees, this horse had no vices. He trusted and loved me and I let him down.

Looking back now, I didn't seem to trust anyone after my divorce, either. I acted out, too. But what do I do about Mickey Gilley? I trusted my choice of owner, she was gentle and had other horses, which he enjoyed the company of. This was for him; he deserved a good home. By now he had been taught a well-collected shoulder in, trot, canter, to lunge and stand when told. This was a necessity and it hurt me so much giving him up, but did I do the right thing? I had to trust myself; he'd settle down. But would he? I was plagued by indecision every day, but didn't have the money to take him back. I didn't even have food in my house – how could I bring him home?

Eventually, I got a call from his new owner and she had hired a professional trainer to help her. She took my suggestion of spending personal one-on-one time with him outside of the training ring. She kept Mickey for a year and then I called the agency to buy him back. I had saved every penny, trying to keep my promise that I would find a way to get him home. I kept my promise only to be told by the adoption agency Mickey Gilley had been shipped to Iowa three days earlier to be used as a trail horse. I cried my eyes out. Three days! I had missed him by three days. I offered double what they donated, shipping costs, etc. They were sorry, but he was readopted – click!

I hope and believe now Mickey Gilley, that funny-looking little Standardbred, is still winning people over with his charm. I also believe the love and trust we had between us lives on. It leaves a gaping hole in both our hearts, but trust was never broken. Life's circumstances just go off course sometimes. I pray that Mickey is being handled nicely. Life is a matter of trust. Without it, we are lost. It builds all relationships, be they equine or human, and cracks can be repaired. Trust in yourself. None of us are perfect. We lose our way sometimes, but we always seem to find a way back to the beginning.

This story is dedicated to all the special horses I have known – especially Mickey Gilley, Frosty, Cash and Rising Star, my new horse. And to John – the man who showed me the way back from the dark.

Tania Roveda

Biography: Tania Roveda. "I worked primarily in stable management and "problem" horses of all breeds. Like everyone else, I mucked stalls to be near the horses and finally got a break when I volunteered to be a night guard and co-manager for the 30th and final Essex Horse Trials, a three-day-event held at the USET Training Center in Gladstone, New Jersey. That's what I consider a vacation! Now I own my one horse and I'm semi-retired from freelance training. I prefer focusing on small, local shows, rewarding myself by living my dream. This story is dedicated to all the great horses I've known."

A Stable Life: A Rider Trades Bridal Vows For A Bridle

Katie and Tyler may be two different species, but they make a great team. And in the end, Katie wanted her horse more than her husband.

Back in 1991, Katie Smith had neither. She was at college and looking for a new competitive mount. She found Tyler in a teeny newspaper advertisement that stood out like a neon sign. Smith hooked up her trailer and went to take a look.

She spotted the roguish, 1,200-pound gray monster the minute she walked in the courtyard, she says, and knew that he would be her next horse. Tyler's veterinary examination confirmed her gut feeling. Because the horse was so powerful and sound, Tyler was the ticket to her dream, a horse capable of upper-level eventing.

Eventing is one of the toughest and most dangerous equestrian disciplines. A three-day event combines dressage, show jumping and cross-country. Dressage tests the communication between horse and rider "on the flat." There are no jumps, but horses must demonstrate submission, communication, subtleness and the willingness to go forward. In show jumping, approximately 12 to 15 fences in an arena must be cleared with as few faults as possible. Cross-country is a jumping course with about 24 to 36 solid and unforgiving obstacles spread over open land, which horse and rider must complete at a very fast gallop.

"Tyler used to fly around the course," Smith says. "He was so sure of where he put his feet, I was never worried; I never got afraid of him, and I never felt unsafe."

Dressage, however, was another story.

Dressage is like ballet for horses, but Tyler would squeal like a pig and swish his tail over his head like a helicopter during his performance. It was frustrating, she says, "He was taking me for a ride like I was a total passenger." Tyler would drag Smith around and bring down their score.

Realizing she was in over her head, Smith found a serious trainer to work with Tyler on a regular basis. Trainers are expensive, so in addition to being a full-time student in college, Smith worked at a restaurant.

In December of 1992, Smith met David Caster at the restaurant. He was home from the Air Force visiting his parents. She and Caster spent three days together, which led to letter writing, phone calls and more visits. "The biggest attraction was his conviction," Smith says. Caster was so committed and forthright about his feelings.

Eight months into the relationship, he proposed. "It was so right from the start, it wasn't even a question," Smith says. Most important to the relationship was Caster's understanding that competition was Smith's life. She said he was intrigued by the massiveness of the whole thing – this young, hard-working woman traveling around the nation competing at upper levels with her horse. Caster supported her emotionally, she says. He helped her at events and, once they lived together, drove the truck and trailer from competition to competition.

Despite his dressage performance, Tyler's jumping talent took them to the highest level of the event world. At 22 years old, she was engaged and competing at the top level. "My life was spinning wildly out of control in a positive way," she says. Smith left college a year shy of graduation to train for the big time.

She made it. In spring 1994, at her first advanced event, Smith finished in the top half. "The jumps were bigger, the speeds faster and Tyler settled in as if it were home," she says. The United States Equestrian Team placed her on the elite rider list, which meant she could be a possible contender for the Olympics. The team sent Smith applications for permission to compete at international competitions and the World Championships. "I remember reading this and thinking, 'Why are they sending it to me?' I think you always have the Olympics in the back of your head, but when you're 22 years old . . . I was just hoping not to make an ass of myself in front of the big guys."

But at the next advanced competition, Tyler got hurt near the last fence; he stopped and wouldn't go forward. At the stable, he walked on only three legs.

Smith learned a very hard lesson: she felt Tyler's injury was her fault, she had wanted so much to compete at the top level, but didn't have the resources to get it done right. Too little money had meant not enough instruction. And her relationship with Caster meant that Smith was spread too thin. She had pushed Tyler too far.

To rehabilitate Tyler, Smith competed in smaller show-jumping competitions and earned prize money (more prevalent at jumper shows than three-day events). Many people noted what a fabulous jumper Tyler was - and thus worth good money.

Smith and Caster had settled in New Jersey at this time, in a town halfway between Manhattan, where Caster wanted to be, and the country, where Smith's heart and horse were. Smith said that in Caster's eyes, Tyler increasingly became a hindrance to the marriage. And he knew Smith could make a valuable profit selling him.

"That's what put it into David's head," Smith says. He convinced her that selling Tyler was necessary because of the money and the time the horse demanded. Smith said Caster pushed, "We have to sell this horse."

Finally in December, 1996, Smith sold Tyler to a prominent lawyer in Virginia. She recalls: "I cried the five-hour trip home; I was so devastated. When I got home, I was in a daze; I didn't feel like I had a purpose." Soon after, Smith began to take a closer look at Caster. "I started realizing why maybe I didn't want to spend so much time with this person."

The relationship headed quickly downhill. "In March, I took my dog, my car and my truck," says Smith, "and split."

Now, at 25, Smith had no college degree, no hope for the Olympics and no Tyler. She became the manager of a fitness club. "It wasn't the path I was expecting," Smith says. "I wasn't thrilled, but it seemed like the right thing to do at the time." Months later, through an old friend in the horse world, Smith was offered the position of head trainer at a beautiful, new equestrian facility in New Jersey's horse country. With the position came a free stall, but no horse. Smith quickly accepted the job.

In February, 1998, Smith received a phone call from Tyler's new owner, who told her he was for sale. He was asking approximately the same amount of money for the horse he paid to Smith. But after much deliberation, the generous lawyer offered Tyler to Smith for a fraction of his original asking price. Smith said she thought that he felt Tyler belonged with her, even though she couldn't afford the original asking price.

"I went down to pick him up," Smith says, "and he was like, 'Mom's here.' He's my boy."

In March, 1999, lightening struck and the Central Jersey farm burned to the ground – and with it, Smith's career with horses. Now, at 28, she is finishing her B.S. in Business Management, supports herself as a veterinary pharmaceutical representative and rides her boy daily. Tyler is past his competitive prime, but he's back where he belongs.

Femke DeCheser

Biography: Femke DeCheser. Born in Amsterdam, Femke rode her first pony on her uncle's farm in Holland. She has been riding ever since. Although Femke sometimes wishes she chose a career with horses, she pursued a B.A. in political science from Colgate University and a M.S. in journalism from Columbia University instead.

Femke lives in the heart of New Jersey horse country, with her husband, dog and new baby. Her horse, Orly, now calls Kentucky home.

Exquisite One

"Hey, why don't you try the new baby?"

I was 18 years old, on Christmas break in the South, far from snow and the grind of pre-veterinary studies. My parents' neighbor was a horse trainer and he was holding out the reins attached to a filly, not yet two years old.

An elegant, doe-like creature, she stood before me like a piece of statuary. Dark copper-gold in color with dapples, she gleamed in the midday sun. A mix of black and white hairs made her mane and tail twin waterfalls of liquid silver. She had dark, intelligent eyes that were fixed on me, and an expression that was curious and friendly. Her name? "Ex," short for "Exquisite."

I was in love before my foot hit the stirrup. She was a serious worker, this filly. There was no hint of youth in her response to the aids. She was sensitive, soft and light in the bridle, and completely focused on her rider. We trotted and cantered around the trainer, a happy pair, lost in each other.

"Wow," he said. "Want to take her home while you're here?"

I did. I rode her the mile or so home, made up a stall fit for a princess, and dreamed of the times we would have together. It was while I was riding her in our pasture a day or two afterwards that she suddenly burst into a heavy sweat and went to her knees. She was colicking. She lay for hours in the same spot, too painful to rise, her gums nearly white from shock. The first vet we called never got the message from his answering service and thus never arrived. The second vet went to the wrong house. At last, as the Milky Way twisted overhead in the night sky and a damp fog settled on the grass, someone came and still more drugs were given. Hours later, she was forced unwillingly to her feet and inched back to her stall. She survived the night, to the surprise of those who had seen her go downhill so rapidly.

Ex recovered. Then I found out why I had been so feverish of late: I woke up a few mornings later with chicken pox. For the next two weeks, bedridden, I watched helplessly as my family cared for the filly.

Every morning they would turn her out in a paddock I could see from my window. She played quite seriously. No bucking or kicking up of the heels for that young lady. She would begin her workout at the trot, stretching into a long frame, keeping to the fence line and 'going large' around the acre paddock. Then she would ease into the canter. This was no gallop, however; round and light, she floated around her imaginary track. Figure eights and changes across the diagonal followed. After several minutes, she would transition to the trot, and seemed to take great delight in lengthening her stride. People driving by would stop their cars to watch the golden horse at play.

Ex was patient with my family's ministrations. Once the blisters on my feet had healed enough that I could bring my pajama'd self to the back door, I bore witness to the following: my father attempting to halter her. He got the noseband on upside down, then flung the remaining jumble onto her face, where it came to rest on her

81

forehead. Loose in the paddock, now, with a knot of nylon web and hardware in her eyes, the filly tilted her nose up to balance the whole mess carefully, lest it fall. She heard me say her name, and turned in my direction. I hobbled to the fence. She trotted gently over and stopped in front of me so I could remove the halter. She shook herself like a dog, and serenely walked off.

At times, she could still be a two-year-old. Mischief was her specialty: squeezing between stall door and wheelbarrow to canter away to freedom, swishing her tail; letting herself in and out of her stall at will, or getting into the feed room, where she seemed more intrigued by the washing machine and the telephone than the grain; plucking laundry off the barn railing to drag it through the dirt with her nose. She had a huge capacity for fun, and could invent games to keep herself amused. Anything left within her reach could suddenly become a toy.

Eventually, I recovered and rode her during the last days of school vacation. By then, the filly had taught herself all she needed to know. When the trainer came to take her back, she lengthened stride for him. It wasn't what they wanted in a Western horse, he said with a smile. "But that's okay, we can fix it."

For two years, I plowed through school as Ex plowed through the deep sand of the show rings of the South. Some vacations I could go to see her, and she would nicker when she heard my voice as I entered the barn. Then, I spent a year or so busy with jobs and internships elsewhere. I neither knew, nor was in a position to intervene, when she was sold. She was still at the same place, helping someone else qualify for Palomino World.

At the end of a summer of working, gearing up for my senior year of college, I found myself once again at my parents' house. What else to do? I went to see the horses. I drove up to the barn I had not seen for over a year. Horses were grazing in the front paddocks. The heat was intense: the air seemed to hang thickly around me, rippling with humidity.

A palomino working on the stubbly grass a dozen yards away perked its ears in my direction.

"What a pretty thing," I said out loud. The horse's head popped up. Something about the face...the body had filled out, and this was a taller, more muscular horse, but...

"Ex!" I called out. I began to run. She, too, launched herself into motion. A few inches from a collision, she abruptly swerved, cantered on, and stopped, her head bobbing, her eyes gleaming, waiting for me to come at her again. We played chase, our old pasture game, for a full 15 minutes before we both grew tired. Then I marched into the barn and met the surprised faces of my old acquaintances with my offer to buy her.

Heads up to those who have grown up reading horse stories: you have no guarantee of riding peacefully into a brilliant sunset. Once I got my horse safely home a year later, her feet fell apart. Instead of riding, I learned to treat hoof abscesses. She would lick the horseshoer's hands gratefully when he would dig out the latest one, relieving the pressure and pain under the sole. I went through six farriers before lucky number seven arrived and was able to keep shoes on her crumbling hooves.

When we could ride, I was faced with the task of retraining my mare. I fumbled my way through it, sometimes crying tears of frustration, always with the latent image of that precocious two-year-old to inspire me. We learned together. We went to schooling shows. Improvement.

When I left for veterinary school, Ex rode a shipping van to our new destination. Then I bought a horse trailer, and we were queens of the highway. I wince now, to think of the thousands of miles we covered in those few years. Always sensible, she traveled well, to the next show, or a new job, or home for vacation. We have never been apart for long.

She is 18 now. Not a gray hair is to be found on her dark muzzle, nor can any loss of condition betray her age. She stands in a northern barn, swaddled in blankets, her gleaming flanks swollen with her first pregnancy. She presides over all, lavishing nickers and attention on her friends, scowling fiercely at any who fail to meet her standards. She owns a piece of my soul. She has cantered through orange groves and apple orchards. She has taught fearful children to ride, and has stamped her petite foot in many a dressage arena, winning over trainers and judges with her willingness and heart. My horse, my friend. I cannot put words together to fully express what she means to me. "You two were meant to be," someone told me once. I have to say it is the truth.

Epilog: A few weeks after I wrote this, Ex gave birth prematurely to an elegant colt, a carbon copy of herself, perfectly formed. A veterinarian, a veterinary technician and a nurse were present. All of our efforts could not save him. We will try again. Next year I hope to be sending you a completely different story.

Stephanie Torlone, DVM

Biography: Stephanie Torlone, DVM . Stephanie resides in Massachusetts, where she practices veterinary medicine and shares her life with two horses, two dogs, and a guinea pig. She and Ex anxiously await the birth of her foal this spring. A new family member arrived recently, in the form of a young Andalusian stallion, Tchao Namorado (his name means "Farewell, Beloved"), as the result of the purchase of a raffle ticket...but that is another story.

Felina's Parting

Felina was the first horse my family owned. She came from the late Johnny Kriz, of Bethany, Connecticut. Her dam was a mare that they received from the University of Connecticut when they sold their horses. Felina was born in the brook that runs through the Kriz Farm property. My parents went to visit the Kriz family one weekend in 1976 and my mother fell in love immediately with "the filly". Johnny put Felina in one of his horse trailers and told my parents to take her home. My parents did not have the money at the time to pay for the mare but Johnny told them they could pay when they had the money. They brought Felina home and began to build their horse barn and pastures.

As I stand here brushing my rose grey Trakehner in the cobweb-covered barn, with the smell of freshly strewed wood shavings still lingering from the night before, I can hear the howlings of the hunt hounds in the near vicinity creating the seven a.m. ruckus about the barn yard. A quick glance outside the sliding door proved my theory to be correct, the sun was relaying brilliant colors across the clear, morning sky; it was definitely a little past seven. An empty sensation poured through me.

Memories of a past October trapped my current thoughts, it had been exactly two years, the true pain of losing a friend walked all over my morning glory. I felt as if I was reliving that Wednesday all over again. Tears quietly embellished my eyes. I walked silently to the corral fence, sobbing in grief, staring deeply at the maple tree, big and strong, standing alone next to the stone wall, with the barbed wire neatly strung above it. The tree is so alive, but buried beneath its caring branches were my memories.

I awoke a bit earlier than usual for a school day; I opened the shade-covered window, allowing the sweet essence of real country air, with a slight detection of freshly spread cow manure from the nearby fields to seep into my room along with the peep of day. The aroma established in my mind that fall was in full swing. I opened the slits in the shade wide enough to see through to discover that the leaves seemed to change into golden reds and oranges over night. They were soon to drop to the ground only to be raked into piles for the children to play in.

Things were routine, Felina was standing under her maple tree, which had been shading and protecting her throughout her 12 years of life.

Each morning Felina would be under her tree without fail. Her one ton, coal black body stood still as day in a relaxed position with her head hung low as if she were sleeping. Nothing abnormal, she always stood in that manner.

Time came to do morning chores. I put on my torn, horse slobber stained, barn clothes and muck boots and headed out the front door of the house. While standing still on the dew dampened lawn I whistled loudly, all of the horses knew this whistle; it signified breakfast or dinnertime. Felina's ears perked forward and she began her morning charge to the barn door.

I strolled to the barn and began dividing up the sweet feed, placing a scoop full in each of the five stalls. The barn door rumbled across its tracks, opening wide enough to allow the horses to come in one-by-one. Felina always being the first to trot proudly into her over sized box stall and the rest following close behind, trotting into their straight stalls. Max, Felina's grandson, was always last to claim his stall.

Felina enjoyed her food and didn't like to be bothered while consuming it. Strangely, I went and sat in her hay manger to intently watch her eat her breakfast. She minded my presence but tolerated it. At first she paid no attention to my being, but once she was finished with every last kernel of corn, and licked her grain tray clean, she turned toward me. She looked at me with her kind eyes and she allowed me to push her forelock to one side of her face revealing her bright white star. I patted her, knowing that she never did like a lot of affection. You didn't dare to hug and kiss her unless she was in the mood to be loved. This morning she permitted me to give her kisses on her pink-snipped nose. I talked to her in a funny, childish voice, telling her how beautiful she had looked at the horse show that past week; although I knew deep down inside that she hadn't been herself that day.

We did so well together, traveling throughout the northeast going from horse show to horse show. We were a team, and usually an unbeatable team. She always knew when it was show time. She would dance around in circles the second she heard the jingling of the harness being pulled from its box. A proud Percheron was what she was. She had a purpose, a job, and she knew it all too well.

With a baby blue mane roll and rosettes tied in her long flowing mane and ribbons tied in her tail, she would put on a breathtaking, exhausting show, working herself into a foamy sweat.

I knew as well as she that something was wrong. She wasn't herself and no one else saw this. No matter how bad she was hurting she would give it all her heart and soul to please the applauding crowd. The roar of the crowd always gave her the stamina she needed to go around the ring once or twice more, pounding her feet as if she were trying to crack the ground.

Showing off wasn't all that Felina did exceptionally well. She loved long trail rides through the neighboring woods. We would go out on the trails for hours at a time. She was most comfortably ridden bareback. Sitting on her big, round body was like straddling a couch. Unlike most horses she wasn't herd bound. She liked to get

85

away from the rest of the crowd at the barn, three of which were her offspring. The trails seemed to be our getaway.

A gentle nudge brought me back to the real world. Time really seems to fly early in the morning. I had school to attend and I didn't want to miss the bus. School began in a little less than an hour, meaning the bus would be cruising down the road soon enough. I patted Felina on the rear end and told her I would see her later.

I changed my clothes and cleaned up for what looked to be just another average day. I was running a bit late so I had to sprint down the quarter mile driveway to the bus stop, making it there in perfect time.

School was school, an ordinary day of 10th grade classes, but indeed an exceptional day in the world of boys. I was falling deeper and deeper into what seemed to be lust with a really nice guy. His touch sent me to cloud nine, not to return for the remaining school day, making me forget those happenings encompassing me.

The bus ride home with a bunch of yelling young adults always made me bus sick. The kids were no longer in the stage of calling each other dumb and stupid but instead they would swear at one another. The typical afternoon ride home.

I was definitely glad to hop down the three steps leading to the paved roadway. Another school day behind me and soon it would be Thanksgiving vacation.

Walking down the driveway was a daily ritual. The stones crumbled beneath my feet, as I lunged forward tripping in a pothole. Leaves on the swaying trees rustled in short gusts of wind. I repositioned my book bag on my shoulder and headed toward the house once again.

My lackadaisical world was interrupted by the sounds of a tractor rumbling across the field. Only dad drove the tractor. The engine shut off and I saw a figure walking across the empty corral. There were two more figures sitting on the porch. I could not see exactly who they were. My mind began to wonder. It's a Wednesday, my father is home, but his car is not. There is a strange car parked in the driveway obviously belonging to the person seated on the porch with a woman who from a distance looked to be my mother. I quickened my pace out of curiosity. Why are all the horses in the wrong corral? Where is my horse?

My dad headed towards me. I could see the anguish in his eyes. Jokingly I asked, "Now what did I do wrong?" Tears quickly filled his eyes. He was holding something from me. Later I would understand that the news he had to tell me would break my heart and practically make me lose my mind. He grabbed me and pulled me close to him as he began to sob.

"Felina is dead," he whispered softly into my ear. A feeling of emptiness filled me and I began to cry hysterically, dropping my book bag to the cold, hard ground. My father pulled me closer to him. The two of us, just stood in the middle of the driveway, weeping in one another's arms. I pushed my father away and began to run toward the house but was intercepted by Shelly, a close friend of the family, practically my second mother. She hugged me and told me that it was too late. My mom joined us, holding me tightly, controlling herself very well.

I turned towards my father and began to question him, " Where is she, Dad?" "Don't go down there," he replied, as he glanced toward the maple tree with an extremely large turquoise blue tarp lying under it.

"No," I screamed. I ran straight for the tarp, not even the fence was enough to stop me as I hurdled over it. A nauseous feeling poured over me as I got within 10 feet of her covered body. I began to walk slowly, one step at a time, closer and closer to her. One front hoof was protruding from under the cover.

In disbelief, I knelt down and pulled the cover from her face. She looked lifeless. I sat next to her and placed her cold head in my lap. A peaceful look of deep sleep was on her face. I ran my hand over her nose. Her mouth was open slightly and her once pink gums were now a pale blue. There was mud and scrapes on her tender face from being dragged across the pasture.

I talked to her in a soothing voice like always. I told her to wake up and to stop playing games and that it wasn't funny. Someone was obviously playing a cruel joke. I wanted badly for her to nudge me at that moment, maybe I would wake up out of this nightmare. There was no way in my mind that she could possibly be dead.

I looked up, finding myself starring into a bright blue sky without a cloud in sight. A warm breeze blew over us. I wasn't going to leave her by herself. She was my friend and friends aren't supposed to go through life or death on their own. I was there for her but now she wasn't going to be there for me. Life was already taking a different perspective.

A shadow appeared behind me, I lifted my head coming eye to eye with my father. I reached out for his hand, he took it in his, and caringly said, "It is time to say goodbye. The sun will be setting soon." He placed Felina's head back onto the damp ground and then pulled me to my feet. I cried out-loud, "I don't want to say goodbye, I love her, she can't be dead." He began to tear me away from her. I could tell that he didn't want to see me going through such pain.

The tractor's engine roared once again as he began to dig the grave. I propped myself up against the stone wall. I felt very weak. As the hole got deeper, water at the bottom began to rise higher. If she wasn't already dead she would definitely drowned in that hole. My father lowered the bucket down next to her body, as he glanced toward me. I didn't want to watch, but I felt I had to.

With a gentle shove, her body fell into the water at the bottom of what seemed to be an endless pit. By the glances I was receiving I could tell he was thinking the same as me. He slowly climbed down off of the tractor as if it was a long hike down and then he walked away, with his head hanging low.

I stood over the treacherous hole, starring at her beautiful body, I almost felt insane. My father was carrying something in his arms as he returned from the barn; it looked to be Felina's red blanket. He jumped down into the grave, straightened out Felina's body the best he could, placing her head on a rock, above the water and then covered her with the blanket.

I interrupted his motions, "Dad, please cut me off a piece of her mane." He removed his army knife from his pocket and trimmed off a locket of mane and handed it up to me.

"Please, go to the house now," he pleaded with me. I turned away and headed to the house, muttering to myself, "Why is this happening?" I went right to my bedroom where comfort was sought, but all I could find were pictures of Felina and trophies and ribbons that Felina had won.

I grabbed the first place ribbon that I had won with Felina at the 1986 New York State Fair and the picture of the ribbon presentation and quickly glanced through the window to see mounds of dirt were now covering Felina.

I rushed out of the house and back to the maple tree yelling, "Stop!" My father halted the machine and saw that I had something in my hand. I held back the tears long enough to say, "Put this ribbon on her halter and place this picture next to her head."

"Are you sure this is what you want to do? I thought that this was the ribbon that meant the most to you," he said questioningly. "Yes, please, just do it," I answered back.

I stepped aside making sure that he did it the way I had asked him to and then watched him finish the burial. I watched as each rock and piece of dirt covered her body, but somehow I knew inside that she was still there with me.

The sun was disappearing in the sky like Felina was in the ground. I knew as I began the journey back to the barn to do evening chores that it would be a sleepless night.

When I realized how chilly it had gotten I could only imagine how cold lying beneath the surface of the ground must be. My nose was numb and my eyes were no longer able to form tears.

Nightmares filled my dreams. Wild dogs pulling Felina's frozen body from the ground by her legs and tearing her limb by limb, as if she were a toy. I awoke the household with screams of terror. My parents came into my room to comfort me until I fell asleep once again. I rose the next morning, leaped out of my bed and scampered to my window only to see the maple tree with a mound of dirt beneath it, where I was hoping to see Felina standing like she had every other morning.

Felina taught my family a lot in her 12 years with us. She afforded us with the opportunity to raise three of her offspring, Diesel, Ebony and Spring. Diesel is still alive today and is now 20 years old. Who knows how much different my family would have been if it weren't for Johnny putting Felina into that trailer.

Stacie C. Lynch

Biography: Stacie C. Lynch. Stacie, originally from Pleasant Valley, New York, is currently an Information Systems Administrator for a Glastonbury, Connecticut based financial software company. She was raised with and competitively shows draft horses and hunter jumpers. She met her farrier husband, Brian, while showing her family's Percherons when she was 12 years old. Their farm, Utopia Percherons, specializes in training, showing and selling young, Percheron hitch geldings for use in competitive six horse hitches. They are currently building their farm in Goshen, Connecticut where they will have several Percherons and Miniature Horses. To learn more about the Lynch's please visit their website: www.utopiapercherons.com.

We are breaking with tradition by bringing you the following poem. While the stories in Horse Tales for the Soul, Volumes One, Two & Three are true stories, the following poem is the first fictional work to make it into the Horse Tales series. While we intend to focus on true stories only, Mike Beville's poem is so touching that I thought it was worth breaking tradition, just this one time. Enjoy!

Horse Hooves On The Ground

He sat easy in the saddle,
His stature long and lean,
And a young man, in the spring of life,
Set out to catch a dream!

His hair as black as a raven's wing,
With shades of cobalt blue,
His eyes wide with anticipation,
At the task he had to do!

Said his folks, "he's trying to rope the wind,"
And to "put his foolish quest asunder."
But his foolish quest was not to rope the wind,
But to rope and ride the *rolling thunder!*

A full moon flew high in the western sky,
As he rode out the eastern gate,
And a south wind blew to warm the youth,
As he turned north to meet his fate!

The morning star lit up the heavens,
Like a jewel in the master's crown,
And the sleeping silence was reverently awakened,
By the falling of horse hooves on the ground!

He rode north through the Monida Pass,
Riding hard for the Montana line,
And he crossed the divide at the Bitterroot,
Between the peaks of ponderosa pines!

In Montana there dwelt a blue roan stallion,
Through the Red Rock Valley he roamed,
His quest? To catch this wild horse stallion,
And to ride the Cayuse home!

The roan was known as a thief in the valley,
Ranchers cursed his name with every word,
For he would trash their fences just at daybreak,
And then would run off with their herd!

The Redman called him *Rolling Thunder*,
As their horse herds dwindled down,
For he sounded like rolling thunder,
When his horse hooves beat the ground!

The youth galloped down into the valley,
Atop his old gray dappled mare,
And on the trail beneath the dapple,
Twas a trace of blood and hair!

And on the shore of Red Rock lake,
He found bright red drops of blood,
And as he followed the crimson trail,
He followed hoof prints in the mud!

In a meadow, beneath a large fir tree,
The great roan horse he saw,
Laying on his side, and bedded down,
In his lair of earth and straw!

His ears alert, yet he didn't run,
As the stranger closed for a closer look,
To find the deadly embrace of a steel trap's teeth,
Locked upon the horse's hoof!

His eyes were wide and filled with fright,
As the stranger stepped down from the gray,
Too weak and tired from loss of blood,
To try and run away!

For six hours he sat and watched the horse,
Time and patience was a must,
For six hours he never moved nor said a word,
To try to win the horse's trust!

Then he hobbled-up his dapple gray,
As the sun went behind the mountain peaks,
And with his saddle beneath his head,
The young man fell asleep!

And when the sun came up again,
His dapple gray he fed,
And with green grass from the meadow,
He lay at the stallion's head!

And as the stallion began to feed,
At it's head the stranger sat,
And with water filled to its brim,
He drank from the stranger's hat!

And before the sun set in the west,
In the last gray hour of dusk,
He removed the trap from the horse's hoof,
And won the horse's trust!

Ten days and nights he watched the horse,
He fed and cleaned his wounds,
Ten days and nights he lived off the land,
And he slept beneath its moon!

Then he awoke one morning,
As the stars danced overhead,
To the sound of *rolling thunder,*
Of horse hooves by his bed!

And when he opened up his hazel eyes,
Beneath the light of the moon he saw,
The blue roan standing at his side,
Fifteen and a half hands tall!!

Standing on all fours, he lowered his head,
Free from pain and strife,
And blew his breath on the young man's face,
As to say, "I'll be your friend for life!"

And when the sun rose in the east,
He eased his saddle upon the roan,
And with the dapple gray following,
He rode the Cayuse home!

And when he rode back into his valley,
His folks heard a rumbling sound,
That echoed like *rolling thunder,*
When his horse hooves met the ground!

Twenty years later,
And now in the summer of his life,
He has himself a family,
Five children and a wife!

His coal black hair is gone now,
Tis salt and pepper gray,
Yet he still rides *Rolling Thunder,*
As he did in yesterday!

Then one day it happened,
The great roan horse went down,
No more to cast his shadow,
Or beat his hooves upon the ground!

And the man knelt down beside him,
As his dying breath blew past his ear,
And he seemed to say, "I'll come for you in December,
In the winter of your years!"

A gray haired man, some years later,
And in the autumn of his life,
All his kids have moved away,
Time to spend with a loving wife!

And when a storm raged outside their cabin,
He turned to her and said,
"That sounds like *Rolling Thunder,*
In the dark clouds overhead!"

Then an owl cried outside his window,
And to him it seemed to say,
"He'll come for you in December,
In the winter of your days!"

An old white haired man lies a dying,
He is in the winter of his years,
His family gathers around him,
Their eyes are all filled with tears!

And in the early hours of the morning,
They found the old man dead,
Then heard the sound of *rolling thunder*,
In the clear skies overhead!

And the sun rose in the morning sky,
As a December wind began to blow,
And on the ground outside his window,
They found hoof prints in the snow!!

Mike Beville

Biography: Mike Beville. Mike first stepped onto the public stage as a cowboy poet in September of 1998, at Loretta Lynn's Ranch in West Tennessee. Since then, he has performed at Cowboy Gatherings in Georgia, Arkansas, Nevada, Westfest in Colorado, Branson Missouri, The Kentucky State Fair, and other engagements too numerous to mention.

Mike is also a freelance journalist, having articles published in "Rope Burns" and in local newspapers. Mike's tape "Cowboy Stories", was released in March of 2001. For more information on buying tapes or booking performances, you can call Mike at 270-737-0263, or e-mail him at Kentuckyskies@aol.com.

Chapter Six
Saying Goodbye

SinJin

Day broke with a bright sun and the promise of a perfect fall day clothed in cool air and blowing leaves. By the time I'd torn myself away from my English paper it was early afternoon, and a dismayingly dark sky spattered droplets of rain. Determined, I pulled on polar fleece breeches and an oversized raincoat, wrapped a hand around a mug of hot coffee and drove out to the barn, listening to hard-core rock music and swallowing the lump in my throat.

SinJin blinked at me resentfully from under a tree as I slipped though his paddock gate. A fine-boned Thoroughbred, he regarded rain with the particular kind of disdain he reserved for dirty carrots and horses he didn't like. He had always borne an astonishing resemblance to Black Beauty, but at that moment he more resembled an oversized Mustang — still gorgeous, but without his usual fit, refined air. His coat was longer than I'd ever seen it; the people at the retirement farm in Virginia had suggested that we not blanket him, and I had complied, concerned for his comfort in his future home.

After searching my pockets thoroughly for peppermints, he allowed me to lead him into the barn and ground tie him outside his stall. As I ran a body brush over his neck, my uneasiness was replaced by calm poise, a numbness echoing the one in my hands that came from the harsh breeze over bare fingers. Possibly aware of my mood, Sinny stood quietly while I tightened his girth, although he hadn't had a saddle on his back in months. He remained motionless while I got on him, a trick that had taken almost the four years I had owned him to perfect.

He walked toward the miles of trails in the same spunky way he always had, unaware that he would never again be ridden. The back and hock problems that had plagued him for a year and a half had finally reached a point, three months before, when our veterinarian proclaimed that Sinny needed a quieter life. His impending retirement was hardly surprising; the 20 year old had led a busy life, but that did little to keep my tears at bay.

That afternoon, I left the reins loose on the path leading to the trail around the lake, closed my eyes and memorized everything about the motion of his quick, rolling walk. I cherished my blindness, knowing how long Sinny and I had taken to build the implicit trust that my visionless state necessitated, knowing how long it would take to build that trust with another horse.

His ears pricked and his gait accelerated as we reached the sweeping path, carved through oaks and maples, that wound around the lake. We'd used the trail for galloping before, and SinJin never forgot a place where he might run. He broke into a jog for two or three steps, melted into a walk before I could reprimand him, and then, as soon as I stopped paying attention, jogged again. When I picked up a light contact he would duck his head into his chest and extend his walk in an amusing parody of a dressage horse. I let him; after all, it hardly mattered what bad habits he picked up in this last ride.

The trail was peppered with landmarks and memories we had amassed over the years: the stretch where I had first trotted him outside, scared to death that my new, high-strung Thoroughbred would take off and leave me hanging from a tree limb; the three-foot high stone wall that had once looked so immense that I'd closed my eyes going over it (I didn't have to worry – Sinny would have exultantly tried to jump the moon if asked); the hill that my friends and I galloped up during a downpour on the way home from a cross-country lesson; the shrub that had once mysteriously swallowed my bright pink polocrosse ball; the rock that told me just when I should start cantering in the interval training we did to get fit; the smooth, soft ground where we would trot when the vet said he was sound enough to ride only on trails. And now, our final ride, because his body had simply had enough, even if he still tilted his shoulder toward the stone wall in an effort to jump it.

He bounced over the dirt, flinging his forelegs and tossing his head, behaving more like a three-year-old just off the track than like a 20-year-old retired horse. His light, repeated tugs on the reins asked to go forward, but his ingrained manners held him back when I told him gently to walk. We were three-quarters of the way home when he finally decided to ignore my soft commands. Oddly, the result mirrored our time together: he broke into a happy gallop, and I, unbalanced and surprised, fell back into the saddle and lost a stirrup. By the time he'd rolled into a flat-out run, I'd regained the stirrup and my balance, and for a perfect moment I crouched over his withers, my hands buried in silky black mane, the wind stinging my eyes and whistling past my ears. I reveled in the coil and release of my horse's flying body, in the way he lowered his neck and lengthened his stride and soared because he loved to run. He'd always loved whatever he'd been taught to do, whether it was to dash through a Western game or gallop after a polocrosse ball or spin over jumps or collect his stride for a nice dressage test, but running was what he loved instinctively.

I insisted that he stop too soon for both of us. After a moment of resistance, he came back to a bouncy canter, head high and body coiled, ready to go faster, wanting to race. Suddenly, I understood that this would be the last time I would feel him gallop, that I would never again win a show jumping course effortlessly, never again see my horse come out of the stall that had been his home for the past four years. Almost back to the barn, I realized that, even though we had stopped galloping long ago, tears still streamed down my face.

The seasons had changed when I saw him next, the longest I had gone without seeing him since I first laid eyes on him. On layover in Dulles, my mother and I had just enough time to scramble out to the retirement farm where he now lived. He raised his head when he saw me, his mouth full of hay, his body round and covered in shaggy hair. I walked up to him and produced a peppermint, and, in return, he snuffled my hand and affectionately butted my arm. He left me mere minutes later, jogging off to bump noses with a small white horse and a lanky chestnut. Seeing him happy made me feel better than when we won our first jumping class, happier than when I'd first galloped him, even than when I'd bought him, my first horse. I missed him the moment I left the farm, but he was safe, he was content, and he would remain that way for the rest of his life. All the ribbons and trophies in the world couldn't have guaranteed his comfort. And had we galloped and jumped together for another four years, I would not have been so happy as I was watching him munch hay quietly in a vast, snowy paddock in Virginia.

Jessie Doernberger

Biography: Jessie Doernberger. "I am a student in Connecticut. I've been around horses since I was young. I currently own SinJin and a six-year-old chestnut gelding, Albany. Albany and I compete in Pony Club, and we're beginning to venture into the world of Combined Training. Sinny is still happy and fat, lazing around Virginian pastures."

Blaze Of Lightning

It has been a year now since Blaze has been gone from my life. It is time now to tell his story, so he will always be remembered.

Blaze was a small palomino pony with a long, thick, light blond mane and tail. He had a dark stripe running along his back from his withers to his tail, faint zebra stripes on his legs and a pale colored stripe through his mane.

I had been looking to purchase a first pony for my young children now that we had moved to a home with land to keep horses. I remember driving down a long dirt driveway through the trees to a small clearing with a house, a few buildings and a tiny fenced-in area where a small, dirty pony gazed with curiosity at us. I knew at first sight that this pony was meant to be a part of our lives.

Blaze was always interested in new things and experiences in his life. When introducing Blaze to Trickster, my chestnut Quarter Horse, the two touched noses and then Trickster proceeded to corner Blaze in the turnout, swung around and nailed little Blaze with several well-placed kicks. Once Trix had become sure the Blaze understood who ruled the turnout, Trix let Blaze become his second-ranked in the chain of command. Blaze was bathed, groomed, wormed and trimmed, becoming a very beautiful little guy. Trickster and Blaze became the best of friends. Every day, the two would groom each other, with Blaze stretching to properly groom his friend.

As a lesson pony, Blaze would often play dumb, as if he had no understanding of what was being asked of him. Knowing he had been a very successful show pony for many youngsters until each child outgrew him, we knew that he was just testing Sarah and Jason as riders. Often, he would be trotting along nicely in the ring, then just stop. He wasn't a vicious pony; he just seemed to feel it was his job to make them become good riders.

Sarah took Blaze to a local barn for some small shows. Sarah was young and small, but at the riding level of older children, so Blaze would be a little pony among a number of horses. Blaze seemed to consider this to be very interesting and captured the hearts of all with his adorable pony routine.

On the trail, Blaze was fearless. I took to ponying him from Trickster when I went riding alone. Blaze met hunters, a group of our landlord's Newfoundlands, cars, car horns and screaming children in passing cars without any worry. He seemed to look with scorn on other horses we sometimes rode with when they shied or spooked.

One time our youngest, Jason, was riding Blaze while my husband and I were on foot. Suddenly, Blaze went quickly trotting away with Jason, having seen some horses in a field up the road. As Bob went sprinting up the road to catch up, there was Blaze with only a strand of wire between himself and four huge black Percherons. When Blaze was sure the four horses knew he was in charge, he brought Jason back to us.

To amuse himself in his turnout, Blaze would entice his unsuspecting victims with this sweet friendly pony act. When the victim was close enough, instantly Blaze became the pony from hell, all teeth and flying hooves. Over the years we saw him do this with dogs, cats, rabbits and people. Although he grabbed and threw the poor animals, Blaze was satisfied to just terrorize the humans, never actually hurting them. When the person was safe outside the fence, they would turn and see Blaze with his innocent, sweet expression on his face.

For a time, we had a large draft horse added to our little herd. Blaze would amuse himself by walking up to Duke, reaching for and grabbing Duke's halter and pulling him around the turnout. I must say that a major event in Blaze's life was when we brought home Waltzing Matilda. She was another outgrown pony, passed along to many places. She was thin and dirty, with overgrown hooves and obviously in need of worming. None of that mattered to Blaze, who was instantly and forever in love with Tilly. Blaze became a little stallion, always keeping himself between Tilly and the other geldings. As Tilly was quite a flirt, Blaze was kept very busy guarding her. Only Trix was allowed near Tilly, but Trix did not love Tilly with the passion of Blaze.

About a year later, we moved to a less secluded area and the three friends lived in a beautiful new barn with large box stalls, pasture turnouts, and the stall opening directly into what became known as the oldster's turnout. We took down the divider between two box stalls and the threesome shared this large space together. Sometimes when I went to the barn for the night's last check on everyone, I would see the three friends all lying down together, warm and snug.

Blaze continued to make our lives interesting with his clever behavior. A favorite trick was to grab a zipper in his teeth and pull the zipper up and down many times. He was always "helpful" when work was done in his turnout or stall. Blaze loved to be ponied by me when I went for a trail ride on Trix. How could I forget the time when we were cantering on a secluded dirt road and Blaze decided he had enough and stopped? As Trix continued to canter, I went right over backwards to hit the ground. Trix was always a gentleman and stopped for me while Blaze gave me his innocent face.

One Halloween, we decided to paint the three friends as Indian War ponies. Sarah rode Matilda, Jason rode Blaze, and I led Trix as we went out to trick-or-treat. Of course, when the three were cleaned of the paint, Blaze did what he loved to do best after a bath. This was to make sure he was being watched by me and then roll in the dirt until he was filthy.

The white plastic fencing that is noted for keeping horses safely separated in their turnouts, Blaze quickly discovered if he put his head through and rubbed his neck back and forth on the middle board, he could pop the board out and let himself and Tilly free to go find greener pastures. We had to run an electric fence wire along the inside of the middle board to bring a halt to this escape plan. Blaze's look of disgruntled surprise when he zapped himself was very comical to see.

The years continued on and Trickster, Blaze and Tilly became retired from active duty. They spent their time grazing and playing together. A Thoroughbred named Chessy became my riding horse. Chessy's stall was next to the oldster's double stall. Chessy was friendly with the threesome, but they were happier to have him in a turnout nearby, rather than having him in with them.

Finally, the day came when Trickster's failing health forced me to let him go peacefully and with dignity to sleep. Blaze was heartbroken and took many months to become his happy self. Almost a year to the exact October day that we lost Trix, the time came for my little friend Blaze to be put down. He had so many health problems and then his lungs partially collapsed, so again I had to let another friend go quickly and painlessly.

As with every horse or pony that I have to say goodbye to, I whispered in his ear a message just for him. I told Blaze how much I loved him and told him to find his friend Trix and run healthy and free in the green pastures of the next world.

Tilly had been frantically calling from the barn for her friend. I brought her out to the field where he lay at peace. As she touched him gently with her nose, she understood that he was gone and never called for him again.

Tilly remained quiet and sad, and looked so lonely in the double stall. I decided to try turning her out with Chessy to cheer her up. Chessy was ecstatic and in love with her and so proud he had his own mare. Tilly seemed much happier and also took up flirting with the two geldings in the next turnout. We put back the divider of the double stall in the spring and brought home a large flea-bitten gray 10-year-old pony named Kelpie. Chessy and Kelpie cannot be together in the same turnout with Tilly, because Chessy does not want to share his love. Tilly is happy again and is queen of the barn, charming all her adoring boys.

Clever, handsome little Blaze of Lightning. You are my friend and Tilly and I miss you so. I have no doubt we'll all be together again someday. I love you, Blaze.

Elizabeth A. Berry

Biography: Elizabeth A. Berry. Born in Natick, Massachusetts, in 1953, Elizabeth was educated at the University of Massachusetts, with a degree in Park Administration. She moved to a small horse farm in Dublin, New Hampshire with husband, Robert, son Jason and daughter Sarah. The dream of owning a horse was realized in 1985 with Trickster. The herd grew with Blaze of Lightning, Waltzing Matilda, Chesapeake Bay and Kelpie. Liz has learned much and been loved so well by many animal friends. She still resides in Dublin with horses and ponies, dogs Little Bear and Claw, cats Pearl and Skylar, and best friend, Bob.

Girl And Horse

The horse bug bit me when I was about three and my father lifted me onto the back of one of his friend's polo ponies. We lived in a wealthy suburb north of New York City, but we were never so well off that we could afford for me to have a horse or the land to keep him on. My mother had to scrape for my riding lessons and trail rides.

After I grew up, married, divorced, and started my own business, I came into enough money that I could afford to do something for myself. However, the choices I made with my life precluded full-time horse ownership in terms of time, and I really didn't want to give up my work, as I enjoyed that also. Then I saw the ad in the classified section of *Hoofbeats,* a monthly publication of the United States Trotting Association. The ad was looking for investors to capitalize a Standardbred horse partnership. I had a soft place in my heart for harness horses (that was why I subscribed to the magazine) and answered the ad. My friends thought I was crazy, investing in such a risky business, but I reminded them of the stock market crash a year earlier. They still thought I was nuts.

So I was driving from New Jersey out to the Harrisburg auction, where the new partners would be looking at experienced racehorses with our trainer. I had never seen so many horses together all under one roof in my life, and spent as much time petting as looking. And we looked … and looked. We saw tall horses, short horses, calm horses and fractious horses. We pored over their pedigrees and racing "lines". We saw them led up and down the aisles. Our trainer poked and prodded them for soundness. By the end of the morning, we had already marked several names in our catalogs that the trainer had recommended we bid on, when he said there was one more on the list. We had just enough time before the bidding started to get to the far end of the barn. Zaxson's caretaker brought him out of his stall. Our trainer began his routine and I went up to his head to say hello. Zaxson sniffed me thoroughly and then lifted his head in an expression that is familiar to most people who work with horses – he reacted to me as if I was an attractive mare. His groom guffawed, "Boy! He really likes her!"

We then proceeded to the ring and started our bidding. To our dismay, most of the horses we had selected rapidly got out of our price range, which at least proved that our trainer was a good judge! We were getting more and more depressed by the time Zaxson came into the ring; however, a few minutes and $25,000 later, we were a bit surprised and happy to find that he was actually ours!

Afterward, I went back to Zaxson's stall to get acquainted and he came to the door immediately, as if he remembered me.

Over the next few months, it became apparent that Zaxson had decided that his career goal was to be some little girl's horse and that he had decided that I was the little girl. This philosophy occasionally clashed with the partnership's goal, which was to race him and make some money, as well as have some fun. There is an expression, "there are a thousand ways for a horse to lose the race, but only one way he can win." We soon started learning the thousand ways, one at a time. He turned out to be difficult to rate, which means that he had his own ideas about how to run the race, which frequently meant he knocked himself out of the race early on and jogged across the finish behind the rest of the field.

I really didn't care if he won or not. I enjoyed holding him while he was being harnessed, or combing his mane and tail, or just watching him work out. Sometimes he would rest his muzzle on my shoulder while the farrier worked on him.

Despite soundness problems and an attitude, he did accomplish a few things while in our partnership. He lowered his race record by two seconds when the trainer removed the hobbles and did win enough races and placed high enough to keep the partnership reasonably solid for a couple of years.

However, we were running a business, despite whatever Zaxson believed it was, and the time came for the partnership to sell him. We had other, more lucrative horses winning for us, and we wanted to start buying yearlings and aim for the big two-year-old stakes races.

I spent most of the last afternoon brushing and talking to him. I combed his mane and tail until they flowed and kept a circlet of hairs to remember him by. He hung his head over my shoulder and I gave him one last hug. He "hugged" back. While we were standing there, I heard a mother and her little girl come into the barn. The mother steered her child past us, saying, "He must love her very much." I was crying silently as I led him to the waiting trailer.

Other horses have come and gone in the years that I've been involved with the partnership. We've had successes and failures, stakes winners and claimers, happiness and tragedy. I often think of Zaxson and wonder what became of his career. I heard that he was racing in Florida in his usual headstrong way, and then lost track of him. I hope people have been kind to him, and that he has found another little girl to be friends with. I'm glad I didn't listen to my money-conscious friends. It taught me that there can be rewards exceeding the risk taken, and I have tried to extend that philosophy to other, more personal areas of my life. I'm glad I took the chance and got involved with a horse.

Adrien Synnott

Biography: Adrien Synnott. "I was born and raised in upstate New York, where I fell in love with horses at the age of three when I got to ride for the first time. I now live on the New Jersey shore, where I perform as a bass player (both acoustic and electric) in theaters and jazz bands. Although I did not choose horses for my life's work, I still remain involved through the Standardbred partnership and collecting and showing model horses."

Apple Jack

Apple Jack waited impatiently outside the paddock gate for his evening meal. Realizing how much the little P.O.A. detested confinement, we had long ago stopped locking him inside his stall and adjoining paddock. Of all the horses, he alone was free to cruise the property. He had more than earned the right.

On this particular evening, as Apple followed my approach, the expression on his face with the spray of long, white whiskers clownishly protruding from an oversized, pink and gray mottled muzzle appeared more morose than usual. Even as a nine year old, when he first came into our lives he always wore a somewhat somber expression. It was his expression, coupled with this quiet, steadfast demeanor, that told me my ten-month search for a suitable children's mount had finally ended.

The details of our first encounter 26 years ago passed through my mind as I stroked the cowlick in the center of his forehead and massaged his lopsided, crested neck which, characteristic of his breed, was topped off with a ridiculously sparse mane of absolutely no consequence.

It was with some reluctance that I drove the 50-plus miles in response to an ad in the paper boasting a "sadly outgrown, bomb-proof pony for sale." But when I arrived and was met by three delightful, giggling young girls who grabbed my hands and excitedly chattered away all at the same time as they led me to the arena to behold their faithful little friend, Apple Jack, I was charmed.

The girls' parents stayed in the background, watching and smiling, and never said one word. The sale began with one of the girls hopping aboard Apple to put him through his paces, from jumping cross-rails to pole-bending, while another of them gave a running dialogue of each event and how well the dapper little pony performed. The third little girl proudly shared their scrapbook of ribbons won and photos of each girl in the show ring performing on Apple. The grand finale came with all three girls sitting underneath Apple, their long, tan limbs entwined around the pony's fuzzy legs as he greedily made short work of the lawn. The deal was set, and I drove home with what would prove to be the buy of a lifetime.

Apple immediately settled into his new responsibility of teaching my two oldest, Lennete and John Lee, to ride. Riding bareback, the kids managed to tumble off, plopping into the sand approximately every 20 steps. No matter, as soon as they slid off, Apple would come to an immediate halt and lower his shaggy face down to them as if to ask what they were doing on the ground. Then he would patiently stand, solid as a statue, while Lennete shimmied her way back onto his back, using Apple's large, knobby knees as a step. After reclaiming her seat atop Apple's too-long back, she would lean over and help hoist little brother John Lee up behind her, whereupon the whole procedure would be repeated.

Apple's tolerance for tiny, barefoot heels and bony little elbows poking and jabbing and little fingers grabbing his thick furry hide as they scrambled aboard was truly amazing. But this remarkable trait was reserved exclusively for children, as very few adults met with Apple's favor. Any child could boldly walk up to him at any time, from any direction, commit every unsafe practice known to horse handling, and never be in danger. Adults, however, were an entirely different matter. Apple would rudely turn his black, spotted rump toward the offending adult as they approached and pretend to be asleep. If they persisted, he would casually move away and re-aim his ample backside toward the intruder, one hind leg cocked, until they got the message.

One day, while my youngest, Pat, and I were out trail riding, Apple's bomb-proof temperament was put to the ultimate test. The mountain trails in Redwood Valley were extremely steep. Some were nothing more than fire breaks. If you weren't going uphill, you were coming downhill. Toward the end of the ride, we headed down the last and steepest stretch of trail and the going was slow indeed. We had stayed out longer than planned. Over-tired, hot and dirty, we were anxious to reach flat ground and home.

Completely absorbed in picking out the safest path, I hadn't noticed that Pat and Apple had fallen a considerable distance behind. Pat's small voice finally penetrated my concentration of our careful decent. Glancing back over my shoulder I gasped and hastily pulled up my gelding.

There stood Apple, head down, chin pinned to his two front hooves, which were firmly planted side-by-side only inches in front of his back hooves. Pat was still sitting in the saddle, small feet still in the stirrups, but had slipped so far onto Apple's neck that he had actually taken hold of Apple's ears in an effort to stay put. As I dismounted and carefully approached, I could only pray that Apple would not explode. The small pony never even flinched as I cautiously lifted Pat from his precarious perch and loosened the girth, freeing Apple from the saddle.

Retirement brought special privileges to Apple and he was quick to take advantage of them, even creating a few of his own. He appointed himself sole keeper of the geese brigade, slowly following their noisy grazing as they clipped at the tall grass in ordered progression across the small pasture. Each afternoon, six geese and one small, gray pony settled down for their siesta upon the knoll in the far corner of the property. Occasionally, he was observed nose-to-nose with one of the half-wild barn cats, briefly sharing a confidence or two. With his oversized, suitcase-shaped head bent low to the ground and his wisp of a tail hanging forlornly behind, he bore a strong resemblance to Eeyore of "Winnie the Pooh."

Once in awhile, mischief would get the better of him and he would deliberately plant himself smack in between Tam and I during the big Thoroughbred's warm-up sessions on the lunge line, which instantly brought the whole affair to a complete standstill until he could be persuaded to move away from the lunging area.

But I think he derived his greatest pleasure from "sneaking" into Tam's stall whenever I brought him out for grooming and exercise. Apple would hide behind the barn wall, peering around the corner until the path was clear to his objective, the stall manger containing delicious wisps of leftover alfalfa, of which he was seldom allowed due to his ever-increasing girth. Once inside, he gleaned every tiny stem. Then he'd turn his attention to the bran bucket and laboriously lick the residue flakes of bran until nary a speck remained. Having thoroughly enjoyed these relished treats, he would stand inside dozing until the return of his tall, elegant friend, Tam. Then Apple would shake his huge shaggy face and emit high-pitched squeals as he hobbled outside as quickly as his bowed, arthritic short legs would take him. I don't think he ever caught on that I purposely left the stall door ajar so he could carry out his naughty adventure.

The sound of gravel crunching beneath Dr. Marc Horrell's truck tires as he turned into the drive brought my thoughts back to the present. Blinking back tears, I gently ran my hand down Apple's tortured, fragile front legs. The past 35 years had taken their toll. The arthritis had progressed to the point that medication no longer alleviated his pain, and he was having more and more difficulty getting around on his crooked, little legs. The time had come to do the "right thing."

It has been several years since his passing, yet I still look for him each time I go out to do chores. The comical little pony with all the wrong sort of conformation was truly the most magnificent equine I've ever known. His gallant heart and kind soul will remain with us always.

Jj Jones

Biography: Jj Jones. "My husband, Jim Russell, and I reside in northern California with our many animal companions. Besides writing and horseback riding, favorite interests include volunteering for Forgotten Felines, a non-profit, feral cat organization (www.forgottenfelines.com), and promoting Jim's invention, the JakeSavr (707) 334-1034. Every year, so many dogs leap to their deaths out of pickup trucks. JakeSavr is a tangle-free device to securely tether one or two dogs in your truck. With JakeSavr, your dog(s) can enjoy a carefree ride down the road. Mostly, we promote responsible pet ownership, for truly, we are our pets' guardians and caretakers, a great responsibility with huge rewards."

Sonny

From the first time I saw him I knew he was something special: he was running around his pasture with a big dead branch of a tree in his mouth, waving it back and forth like a matador.

After I bought him as an unbroken two year old, I brought him to the boarding stable where I kept my "kids' horse." The day he arrived, I turned him out in the big arena with all the jumps in it. He took one look at the jumps, ran over and jumped over one. From that day on, he would jump a little course of his own design every time I turned him out in an arena with jumps.

At two and a half years old, having grown tired of my repeated attempts to break him to the saddle, Sonny was being impossible and refusing to do *anything* I asked. I called my extremely experienced trainer friend, who loaned me a very soft, very long cotton rope so I could tie Sonny's one foreleg to his stomach with a bowknot. Theoretically, he would feel his leg tied, would panic and fall down in the sand arena. I was supposed to go over to him, untie the bowknot and he would be obedient and willing from that time on. Not so! Sonny just grazed on the grass at the edges of the arena *on his knees*. Since he wasn't fazed by this and we only had one arena where we were keeping our horses at the time, my 21-year-old daughter Tina started riding the "kids' horse", ZaBoe, in the arena. Sonny decided to chase ZaBoe even though his one foreleg was *still tied to his stomach*. Sonny was running faster and faster and Tina was galloping around the arena as fast as she could on ZaBoe. Sonny couldn't catch ZaBoe, so he took a short cut and jumped one of the jumps *on three legs*. Luckily, he gave up the chase shortly after that.

He liked people whom he considered "the entertainment." His favorite "trick" was to grab my shoelaces with his front teeth and yank them straight up, knocking me on my butt. I took to wearing boots to groom him. Then he would grab my jeans pant leg for the same "trick." I had to groom him in boots and breeches to be safe. He would constantly try unsuccessfully to pick me up with the back belt loop on my breeches.

He amused himself by moving, with his teeth, the tack on the tack wall, the supplies in the wash rack, the grooming tools (while I was using them). Out of desperation, I would hang a towel over the noseband of his halter to keep him busy.

Whenever he found a water trough, he would put his whole face in until the water was over his eyes and then play "tidal wave" with his head until all the water was out on the ground.

106

Sonny was smarter and had a bigger imagination than ten horses put together. He wasn't afraid of anything. If something looked scary, he would walk right over and investigate it.

Tina showed him in hunter/jumper classes for years and I qualified him for the volunteer unit of the State Park Rangers. Sonny loved patrolling at the lake, since he got to meet lots of admiring people and to go on many long trail rides.

Eventually, my daughter moved to Alaska and my multiple sclerosis got too severe for me to ride safely. I sold him so he could have an interesting life.

Many months later, I hesitantly parked at the very edge of the dirt road. I had stopped to just look at his handsome self, although he was at the far end of his new owner's huge pasture. Recognizing my car, Sonny came galloping to the fence with the same enthusiastic, proud gait he had always had, knowing he was gorgeous, greeting me loudly all the way. He loved me, even as sick as I was.

It had been a little more than a year since I had seen his curiously devilish face with the blaze turning into horns above his eyes. Looking into his intelligent eyes, I remembered his mischievous personality and how eager he had been to jump.

It quite distressed me that his feet were being neglected and his skin allergies had returned.

Feeling noticeably lightheaded and miserably fatigued, I drove away. Sonny didn't know that this was the last time he would ever see me. Saying goodbye is too painful. I vowed to never visit him again.

Suzy Hopkins

Biography: Suzy Hopkins. "Since I can no longer ride because of multiple sclerosis, I get my horse fix in other ways. I work as a ground trainer at Saddle Pals Therapeutic Riding Center in Orangevale, California. I have been an equine photographer for 16 years, working horse shows, polo games and doing portraits. I have also been a horse/people trainer for 30 years and have created the successful eight-week course *Breaking Your Horse to the Saddle Yourself*." To reach Suzy Hopkins or Pony Express Equine Photography for a variety of notecards or for the course, *Breaking Your Horse to the Saddle Yourself,* call 1-800-419-7436.

The Passing Trilogy

As the owner of a boarding facility in Massachusetts I have been fortunate to meet and care for many remarkable horses over the years. Below is a trilogy I wrote to honor three of these special equines.

Shy-Guy

Shy was my wonderful Ponderaia's Shy-Guy Shylo who passed at 34 from cancer. Proud to the end he pranced, head held high, in each of his many parades. His favorite activity was galloping down the beach and he looked forward to his very own ice cream cone on the return trip home. He will be forever missed.

For Shy-Guy

He was not born of royal blood,
There were many more Noble than he.
But within him lived a precious soul,
Which I was fortunate enough to see.

The best of conformation was not his,
Nor was a coveted Pedigree.
But we shared something far more precious,
The bond between him and me.

Shali

Sunraf Shalimar, an Arabian mare, was 24 when she succumbed unexpectedly to colic. Christine, Shali's owner, befriended me while Shy was deteriorating as her other horse, Gil, had the same condition. Therefore, it was a shock to everyone when Shali suddenly became ill instead. At this writing thankfully, Gil is still going strong!

For Shali

So hard to lose the good ones,
Those special friends we've known.
So sad to close the chapter,
When *Great Spirit* calls them home.

We'll know that they're still with us,
By the storms that crash on high.
Their hoofbeats are the thunder,
We'll hear them gallop by.

We'll see their eyes flash in the lightning,
Your *Shali* and my *Shy*
We'll feel their breath on the summer wind,
And know their spirits did not die.

Shami

Shami, whose full name was Shamalot, was in his early 30's, a victim of old age. His rear legs would no longer support him. The decision to put him down came from the deep love that his human companion Jane, one of my best friends, had for him.

For Shami

Shami you were beautiful.
I loved you as my own,
Those years you boarded here and called The Ponderaia home.

Shami you were beautiful.
Your life was long and good,
Until your body weakened and your owner understood,
With no further way to help you she had to let you go.
You were her first and special boy.
She'll always miss you so.

But memories are forever and will always keep you near,
She'll close her eyes and call you and you will still be here.

Shami you *are* beautiful as you gallop on alone
To meet those gone before you in your new forever home.

Laine Raia

Biography: Laine Raia. Laine is the proprietor of The Ponderaia, a boarding/leasing facility in North Reading, Massachusetts. The Ponderaia, a takeoff of the old Ponderosa TV cowboy show, focuses on the mature rider. Laine has ridden out after wild horses on Bureau of Land Management land in both California and Wyoming. A multiple horse owner, licensed instructor and English rider, Laine also enjoys tacking up Western for gallops on a nearby beach. Laine enjoys writing and is currently working on a book about Shy-Guy Shylo's long and interesting life. You can read her story "Tough Guy" in Horse Tales for the Soul, Volume One, and "Moonlight Horses" in Volume Two. Laine can be reached at laineraia@attbi.com or by calling The Ponderaia at 978-664-5322.

Movie Star Horse

Our son taught riding lessons and word got around about our calm and gentle horses. One day, we were approached by a college student who was going to make a movie for one of his classes. He wanted to use one of our horses. Another student would be riding the horse and acting in the movie. This meant trailering the horse several days over the Jamestown Bridge, and waiting while they were filming the movie. Our son was willing to do that, and was surprisingly excited.

The actor who was to use the horse was dressed in a Tarzan suit, perched up in a tree, ready to jump onto the horse and ride away. As he went to leap, he slipped and tore his Tarzan suit to a very unpresentable condition. Our daughter, who had decided to go with her brother this particular day, was there when it happened and broke up laughing. That marked the end of filming for that day, but not the end of my stories.

Our daughter was still a student in high school and one day a substitute teacher walked into her classroom. She realized it was the Tarzan actor who played in the film where our horse was used. Of course, our daughter broke out laughing again and when he recognized her he happily obliged to tell the class in detail what had happened. The whole class had a jolly good laugh.

The name of the movie was "Eyes" and it was shown at URI, the University of Rhode Island, as a class assignment with an invitation only.

Another college girl heard about our horses and called to ask if she could use one and needed someone to just lead her around. She could not ride, but she wanted to be Lady Godiva at a homecoming celebration. Our son walked her around on our horse for about two hours, attracting lots of attention. He had made her a happy person that day which she'll long remember, and so will our son!

Alice Johnson

Biography: Alice Johnson. "I was brought up to be afraid of horses because my mother was afraid of horses. Two weeks after buying our first horse, I invited a friend to ride and the first thing she said after she saw me handle the horse, was, "You can tell you have been around horses most of your life," and I said, "Yes, a total of two weeks." I was a leader of the Hoofbeats 4-H club in Wakefield, Rhode Island, for a number of years, and spent hours making riding jackets for my tall, thin son and daughter. I started out as a bookkeeper and bought the grocery business from my employer when they wanted to retire. I retired from that in 1951 when my first son was born. I stay busy now that the three children have flown the coop, quilting, knitting, sewing and painting. I am still active in 4-H, helping to raise money for their state program. I was inducted into the Rhode Island 4-H Volunteer Hall of Fame in 1999 and I am a young 81-year-old lady!"

Chapter Seven
When Life Is Anything But Fair

Captain Crunch

His chin was prickly, like an old man's beard, as I gave him a kiss. He nuzzled my shoulder and the warm air from his big Thoroughbred nostrils warmed the back of my neck. It sent goose bumps down my spine. I especially loved his muzzle after it had been clipped because it reminded me so much of black velvet. I had clipped him just the week before, but his whiskers were beginning to emerge again. It didn't matter; it was the dead of winter anyway. He wasn't getting ready for a show, or a clinic, or even a lesson; he was fighting for his life.

Nothing was harder for me to do than to sit there with my best friend, and know there was nothing I could do to make him better. At least on the rare occasion when he was lame, there were things I could do to help him. But now, no amount of poultice, or Vetroline, or Bute could help Crunch. Colic was his enemy, and it was teamed up with old age. Despite the fact that he was in his mid-20s, looking at him you'd think that he was still perfectly suited to be at the track or some Thoroughbred breeding farm in Kentucky, rather than at a hunter show barn. I swear he suffered from what we jokingly called "track flashbacks." These always seemed to occur during the busiest part of our warm ups at shows. In fact, when he didn't act up in warm up, I'd worry that the show wouldn't be a success! But that was the type of humor and personality that Crunch exuded that made me love him so much more.

My bond with Crunch was like no other I have ever experienced. Despite his muscular, 17-hand frame, he never intimidated me. I truly felt at home on him, as if we were destined to be together. Even if I was having a horrible day, all I needed was to hear his deep nicker as I entered the barn, and all my troubles and tribulations would vanish. I swear he recognized the sound of our car, because every day, without fail, I'd hear him welcoming me to the barn before I even saw his face. I could stand in the parking lot for ten minutes, and his incessant whinnying would not stop until after I had gone in to his stall and given him a kiss. That made me feel so loved.

I love to think of Crunch as a "horse of firsts". He was the first horse I truly fell in love with. The first horse I won a Seasonal Grand Champion award on, which was the Thomas School of Horsemanship Seasonal Grand Champion award for Primary Equitation. And, sadly, he was the first horse I ever lost.

I understand now that the humane thing to do was to let Crunch go peacefully. The vets explained that colic surgery on a horse of his age was risky, although it could be attempted. They also said that even if the initial surgery had been a success, there was a good chance that Crunch would not have the strength to overcome the anesthesia. Early the next morning, Crunch was put to sleep. After a long frigid night of warming IV bags and just sitting beside him trying to imprint his every last detail in my mind forever, I lost my best friend.

Even when I think about him now, I cry. Sometimes it's because I'm remembering all the amazing rides, and equally amazing moments of silence we shared. Like when I used to concentrate on the sound of his breathing at shows to relax me between classes. Sometimes I cry because I'm remembering that mid-December night, when my world changed so drastically. But while I'm thinking about him, I can still hear his breath. I can still see his sides moving in and out with a grace that only he could capture in the simple art of breathing. And sometimes, I get goose bumps, like I had the night I spent with him when he buried his nuzzle deep into the crook of my neck. But most of the time, I cry because I know that all of those things are a memory, and I'll never feel his soft velvet nose on my neck again.

In times like these, your friends become so much to you. When I finally had enough strength to return to the barn and face his empty stall, it was my friend's shoulder that I cried on, not my empty hands. Most people were touchy with the subject, and it was obvious that they didn't want, nor understand how to bring it up. After all, what do you say? My friend Amanda was such a help to me. She had been through the experience of putting a horse down, and she knew how uncomfortable it was for me to talk about it. She knew that saying "I'm sorry" wasn't enough. She knew that all the apologies in the world couldn't change how I felt. She also knew that silence was nice. Just to sit with someone who went through all the same emotions that I was going through was so comforting. Thank you, Amanda.

Another friend told me some news that did make me feel a bit better. She told me that she had seen Crunch turned out the morning that he got sick, one day before he died. She said that despite some snow, he was running around as usual, bucking and playing with his buddies. It was reassuring to know that he had one last day to be with his friends and one last beautiful morning to spend in the field having the time of his life. He was so impressive when he was turned out. I could just sit and stare forever at his glistening coat, and listen to the methodical pounding of his hooves. Sometimes his speed impressed me so much that I wondered why he wasn't more successful as a racehorse. He had a tattoo, but we never investigated it. It didn't matter to us if he had won any money at all, because he was priceless to us just the same.

112

I like to remember Crunch as my friend had described him that day – as a healthy, happy horse, just loving his life. I know that one day I too, will get very old and leave this earth, but I also know that I will see Crunch again. I'll walk into the barn just as I always did, and he will nicker, and bury his muzzle in my shoulder. I'll kiss him, and we'll have all of eternity to make up for lost time.

The lessons that Crunch taught me, in and out of the saddle, were amazing. I learned that you need to love with all your heart, every day of the week. Cherish every moment that you spend at the barn - even those that are less than ideal. Make sure your horse knows you love him, and most importantly, never forget about those that have left us. They aren't that far away if you keep them in your heart, as I have kept Crunch.

Michelle Riggs

Biography: Michelle Riggs. "As a member of the class of 2002, I graduated from General Douglas MacArthur High School, and will attend Johnson & Wales University in the fall of 2002, majoring in Equine Business Management. I would like to thank my "family" at the Thomas School of Horsemanship for the overwhelming support and love they have shown to me over the last 13 years. A special thanks to Judy Galterio and Nancy Mayall for helping me find the strength to always go on, and the courage to follow my heart. You'll never know just how much you mean to me."

Cherish The Time

In the 14 years I have been alive, I've had lots of losses. My Grandpa died when I was six, and at eight, I was in a car accident where my younger brother died. I was very close to him and it hurt to have an empty house again. No more yelling or Ben running after me, screaming. Some days I would sleep in his room and we would talk all night about school, or what we were afraid of; no more of that.

I never rode horses except at fairs, but I've been around them all my life. The neighbors of my grandparents' farm had two "elephant" horses, Jimmy and Jerry. The three of us had grown up together, and we were like best friends. They never worked a day in their lives, but they respected me. The same year as the accident, my family and I decided that I could take riding lessons.

I had a great time for the first two years, winning ribbons at local shows. My mom asked if I would like to take lessons from a former neighbor, Frances, and I jumped at the chance. We went by her house on the way home from a riding lesson. There, I met Mercedes, a black Thoroughbred, and Beckett, a chestnut Thoroughbred/Belgian cross. Mercedes had been abused before she was purchased by Frances. On one eye, her eyelashes were gone, and she wouldn't trust anyone. Frances slowly earned her trust and began competing in cross-country events. Beckett was bought by Frances' stepfather and was a handful of trouble. When some workmen were making a shelter, they tested a gate and Beckett ran right through it.

When I knew Beckett, she was only 12 and broken of all her bad habits. I thought greatly of her and Mercedes. I remember Frances had to get something and left me alone with Mercedes. Her head towered over me, and her lip hung loosely. The whole time I just stared at her, gently petting her neck. From that moment on, I knew that I wanted to have a horse and wanted to work with them forever.

Summer came and Frances took Mercedes to a local cross-country show and the tall black horse never came home. Instead, she was taken to an equine hospital in Guelph. One of her back hooves had over-reached and punctured above her fetlock. It didn't look good. She had good days and she had bad days, but in the end, Mercedes was put down, so Frances came home empty-handed. Frances bought another horse, which her daughter named Jasmine (now called Minx), so Beckett had a field mate.

A month later, Beckett became sick. The huge chestnut was lying crumpled on the ground, unable to get up. A horse that I had came to know and love as a friend and knew that would never want to lose a fight without trying was losing the fight for her life. After a week, I came home from camping with my younger cousins and my mom hit me with bad news: Beckett had died. I cried non-stop for days afterward. I lost my brother and now a beloved horse; life didn't seem fair.

A couple of days later, my mom told me that Frances was stroking Beckett when she died and no more then a second later, she saw a vision of Mercedes and Beckett meeting in the clouds, rubbing noses. She says that it wasn't a dream, or a wish – it felt like it really happened.

Eventually, my family decided to buy me a horse of my own. We were having trouble finding one, so we leased one named Mary Poppins from a nearby stable.

She may have seemed wild to people who didn't know her, but she cared for me, and I cared for her. We were the perfect match – both skinnier than most and stubborn. She loved to jump, but after a couple of jumping lessons, she usually went lame, so we just did flat work, which she hated.

Even though she was in her early 20s, Mary Poppins had a very strong personality. I once let a horse on the other side of the fence sniff my hand to show that I didn't have a treat and M.P. was curious to see if I did really have any treats. As I had two horses sniffing my hands, I was carefully watching the other horse, just in case she tried to bite me. M.P. put back her ears back and bit my fingers! She was mad because she thought I was giving away her treats!

Despite all her little problems, I loved and cared for her, and she cared for me. She would listen to me and we would play in the field, with her trying to follow me everywhere. She was very unique, and whenever she saw Tupperware containers, she knew that meant treats, so if she was mad at you and you brought out the Tupperware, she instantly forgave you.

Mary Poppins went back to her stable at the beginning of May of this year. Even though she is gone, I see her most weekends and I know she looks forward to seeing me, even though I share her treats with every horse.

I have been around horses all my life and they mean everything to me. Horses have taught me almost everything I know, but the most important thing that they have taught me is that everyone will leave you at one time or another, but you have to cherish the time you spend together and they will always stay in your heart, so they will never really leave you.

I have had many hard times in my life, maybe more than most my age, but I can guarantee that through the rest of my life I will always have a horse at my side that will help carry me through the bad times with a mane to cry on, and be their best through the good times, with their head high and proud.

Stephanie A. McQuaid

Biography: Stephanie A. McQuaid. Stephanie is 14 years old and lives in Bethany, Ontario, with her parents, dog Sadie, cats Rosemary and Frisbee, and rabbits Chocolate Bunny and Allie. Stephanie has been riding since she was eight, but had been longing to ride them ever since she could remember. In May of 2001, Stephanie bought and began training a five-year-old Arab/Quarter Horse cross-named Trudi, who is boarded at Fleetwood Stables under the management and supervision of Frances Ford. She loves to write, especially about animals and particularly about horses.

Ginger And Elizabeth, Part Two

For those of you who have read Horse Tales for the Soul, Volume One, you already know most of the story of Ginger and Elizabeth. For those of you who have not read Volume One yet, I suggest you read the first installment before continuing.

It was 4:00 p.m. when Elizabeth's mother phoned.

"Elizabeth had a bad dream last night," she said. "She dreamed that you gave Ginger away before Tuesday, when we are supposed to pick her up and bring her home."

"There are no two creatures on earth that belong together more than those two," I assured her. "Wild horses couldn't convince me to give that horse to anyone else but Elizabeth. Tell her everything is fine and I'm looking out my kitchen window at Ginger running the fence line with the "boys". She is really looking good and I know the whole neighborhood is going to be thrilled when Ginger finally gets to go home with Elizabeth."

Of course, they will all be thrilled. Since Ginger arrived in the bed of a pickup truck last January with more bones sticking out of her carcass than you could find in a butcher shop, I had worried. I worried that after so much neglect and at her advanced age she wouldn't make it. I worried that she would die without knowing the love of a devoted child; without knowing that life could be good, in spite of the bad side that she had experienced her whole life.

But all my worrying was about to end. For the past winter, Ginger had become the project of the entire neighborhood. Even the retired farmers found a soft spot in their otherwise jaded hearts for this old mare. I think the farmers recognized a piece of themselves in Ginger; the part of themselves that was used up and tossed to the side by life, simply because of their age. I think they were all secretly rooting for her recovery, just as I was. Ginger was now fat, feeling great, enjoying all the attention from the local farmers and students who brought her bags of carrots and friends who were amazed at how quickly she was filling out.

"For a horse of her age, Ginger is looking like a movie star," I said to Elizabeth's mother. "In fact, she is looking so great that Frank has fallen in love with her. Frank is that huge, great-looking Thoroughbred that was donated to the farm from the East Coast. He follows her around like a puppy dog. It is funny to watch them together – she, an aged large pony and he, this huge, spry, young 16-plus hand majestic Thoroughbred off the track. Please tell Elizabeth her horse is fine and I was just heading out the door to feed when you called, so I had better get out there before they start a riot!"

We finished our conversation and I headed to the barn. As I always did, I fed the inside horses first and then placed feed in the stalls of the outside horses. Once that was done, I would open the large back door of the barn and let "the boys" and Ginger in. They knew where their stalls were and they would make a beeline for their respective houses, where they knew dinner awaited them.

After opening the back door, I returned to doing my chores. "The boys" all belonged to me and Ginger was still one of my own until tomorrow, when she would be going home with Elizabeth. They all knew the routine and there was no need to baby-sit them. However, this particular afternoon, I realized that Ginger wasn't in her stall. I called for her and then noticed Frank wasn't inside, either. Laughing to myself, thinking that they are so in love, they can't even be bothered to eat!

I headed out the back door of the barn to find the two of them standing side-by-side about 50 feet from the back door. I laughed and said, "Get in here you two!" Both their heads turned toward me, but no one moved. Finally I yelled to Ginger, "Come!" She faithfully went to take a step and then I realized that one of her front legs was swinging. It was moving as though there were no bones in it. I was horrified. This couldn't be happening – not now!

I headed toward her, only to find that Frank wouldn't let me get within 10 feet of her. He knew something was wrong with Ginger, and he was going to protect her to the death if that is what it took. I left them in the field together, knowing that Frank would be with her as I ran to phone the vet.

"This is Bonnie at Whitehall," I said urgently. "I think Ginger has broken a leg. I need you to come out and fix this."

My old, seasoned vet replied, "Bonnie, you knew when you brought her in that she was old and had brittle bones from all that neglect. If she has broken a leg, there is nothing we are going to be able to do for her."

By this point, my normally calm demeanor was long gone. I was screaming at him over the phone. "Look, she can't die now, not now. She finally has a child of her own to care for her. The whole neighborhood has been rooting for her to make it. She can't die now, not when she is so close to having the life she deserves. You have to fix it."

"I'll come, but I can't make any promises," he said.

In a strange twist of fate, Connie pulled into my driveway a few minutes later. It was Connie who had called me in January to tell me that a man she knew was in the middle of a divorce and was leaving town and just remembered that he had a horse standing in a field that he forgot about. Did she know of a place he could dump her? It was Connie who came with that man to deliver Ginger in the bed of his pickup truck on that cold Saturday morning. It was Connie who was there to see how Elizabeth immediately fell in love with this old horse, even though you could see her entire

117

skeleton. And now, it was Connie who was going to be there to see how the story ended.

I asked Connie to stay at the back door of the barn and keep an eye on Ginger and Frank while we waited for the vet. I had a phone call that had to be made.

"This is Bonnie calling from Whitehall. I have some bad news." I said after Elizabeth's mother answered the phone.

"What's the bad news, Ginger and Frank ran off together?" she said, laughing over our previous conversation.

"No, Ginger appears to have broken a front leg while running the fence line this afternoon. It looks bad. The vet is on his way out and the only reason why I am calling is to let you know that if there is nothing that can be done for her, the vet is going to want to put her down. Knowing how much Elizabeth loves Ginger, I wanted to call to let you know what is going on and to let you know that if you want to avoid this nightmare, you can tell Elizabeth that I did give her away after all and let her hate me. Frankly, I would rather she hate me than have to face this."

After a pause on the phone, Elizabeth's mother replied, "No, I'll tell her the truth."

As terrible as I felt at that moment, I was glad to hear that she was going to be truthful with her daughter. "If you want to give Elizabeth a chance to say goodbye, now is the time, as the vet is on his way out." By this point, I could barely contain my tears. I kept telling myself, this isn't about you. This is about Ginger and Elizabeth and whatever you have to do to make this day easier for them, you do it.

"I'll call my husband and we'll be over as soon as we can," Elizabeth's mother said.

With that, I promised her we would wait and I hung up the phone. The vet arrived a few minutes later. Together, we headed out into the field. Frank lunged at us with his ears pinned in an attempt to protect his beloved Ginger. I asked the vet to wait while I clipped a lead line to Frank's halter and put him up in the barn.

When I returned, Connie and the vet were standing next to Ginger. "There is nothing that can be done for her," the vet said. "The leg is shattered. She has no solid bone from the shoulder down to the top of her hoof. It is all just fragments now."

I knew he was right, but I just couldn't let go. "Can't we insert pins or something?" I pleaded. "No," he replied. "Can't we hang her in a sling for six weeks and let the bones mend?" By this point, I knew I was fighting for her life and I wasn't going to give up easily. I couldn't. "Can't we take her to the University? Maybe they can do something for her."

Connie came over to me and put her arm around my shoulder. "Let it go. You and I both know there is nothing that can be done for her. Let the vet put her down."

"Nobody is going to touch her until Elizabeth gets here. I promised," I barked at them both.

The vet said impatiently, "I have other calls to make and we know there is nothing we can do for her, so let's get on with it."

"Is she in pain?" I asked. "No, she is in shock," he replied. "Then get away from her," I demanded. "Elizabeth is not going to be cheated out of saying goodbye."

By this point, Connie was crying, the vet was angry with me and I was holding it together by a thread, knowing that Elizabeth was going to need all the help she could get when she arrived.

It was a few minutes later that the familiar station wagon pulled in the driveway. The entire family had come – mom, dad, Elizabeth and her younger brother. They all walked over to the field fence to peer in. Without hesitation, Elizabeth scurried over the fence. She was an agile nine year old who loved all horses, but especially Ginger.

Ginger stood in the field alone and when I realized that Elizabeth's parents were not entering the field, I did. "No one should have to face this alone, especially not Elizabeth," I thought to myself.

Elizabeth and I hugged in the field. I hugged her tightly, hoping that I could somehow take away all that pain and hurt. "Elizabeth, I'm so sorry."

"It's okay," Elizabeth replied in a soft voice as she headed over to her dear friend. She threw her arms around the mare's neck and hugged her harder than I have ever seen someone hug another.

"Ginger, I love you, but if you have to go now, I understand," she said with a quiet wisdom that I have rarely witnessed in my life. I could feel something die in me at that moment, something deep in my soul. My heart broke over Elizabeth's sorrow and she wasn't even my child. I couldn't imagine the heartache that a parent must go through when they witness their own child endure the cruel tricks that life can play.

Ginger rested her head on Elizabeth's shoulder and the two embraced for what seemed like an eternity. "Goodbye Ginger, I love you," Elizabeth said, and with that, she turned and quietly walked out of the field. Within a minute or two, the station wagon disappeared out of the driveway and I was faced with the reality of the vet standing at the back door of the barn, impatient, with needle in hand.

"Why don't you go into the barn? I can take care of this," he said, trying to show some compassion now that he understood how much Elizabeth loved this mare. "No, I'll hold her while you give her the shot. She deserves to have someone with her who loves her," I replied. By this point, my heart was as shattered as Ginger's leg. I was just going through the motions now, doing the right thing as I always tried to do. I have learned over the years that sometimes in life, that is all there is and this was one of those times for me.

It all went very quickly. "When you see her start to lean, let go and step back," the vet warned. He said she would be dead before she hit the ground, because the drugs worked that quickly, and he assured me there would be no pain.

"I'm sorry it all turned out this way," the vet said and soon he was off to his next call. There was a storm rolling in and Ginger would spend the night in the open field alone until the renderer could come in the morning.

Connie had two children and although I had none, without saying a word, we both understood the injustice and cruelty of what we had just witnessed. How unfair it was to Ginger and to Elizabeth. Ginger was so close to finding happiness. She had survived starvation and neglect. She had become the poster child for hope in our barn. Everyone was rooting for her to make it, to find a perfect home, to have the good life that she so deserved, and we were just one day away from making that a reality. The long, hard road was almost over for Ginger – and then this.

As the sun was setting, my best friend, John, pulled in the driveway. He was British and had ridden race horses on the tracks in England in his youth. He had witnessed the transformation of Ginger and Elizabeth over the winter and was rooting for them to make it as much as I was. The three of us quietly finished up the barn chores for the evening and headed into the house. By now, the sun was down and it was pounding rain when the phone rang. It was Elizabeth calling.

"Bonnie, do you think you could save me a locket of Ginger's hair so I would have something to remember her by?" Elizabeth asked in a quiet whisper.

"Sure Elizabeth, I wou d be happy to do that for you." I answered. "I'm sorry you had to go through this oday." It was all I could do to stop the tears.

120

"It's okay," she answered, in that same calm manner I had witnessed in the field this afternoon.

After hanging up the phone, I put on my rain gear and wellies. "Where are you going?" John asked.

"Elizabeth wants a locket of Ginger's hair and I'm going out to get her one," I answered.

"You can't go out there; it's pitch dark and raining," John said. In the end, the three of us headed down to the barn, turned on the lights and John, with scissors in hand, disappeared into the darkness out the back door of the barn. Connie and I waited in the barn office for what seemed like an hour. Fifteen minutes later, John emerged from the pouring rain with both arms filled with horsehair.

"What in the world did you do out there?" I asked.

In the typical fashion that one might expect from a man with four children of his own, John answered, "I didn't want to take the chance that Elizabeth wouldn't have enough hair to remember Ginger by, so I cut off all of her mane, tail and forelock!" For a brief moment, Connie and I smiled. We both understood that his intentions were completely sincere, and that he felt as much sorrow over this loss as we did.

The three of us spent the next two hours at my kitchen table, combing and braiding the hair that John had gathered. Fortunately, I had a box of small horse dolls and we fashioned them into mobiles with the hair, making them into hanging baskets and other things that would allow Elizabeth to remember her friend in a loving way. Sometimes in the middle of a storm, you have to hang onto whatever you can and that night, I was grateful for my friends.

Elizabeth, in typical nine-year-old fashion, was back at the barn two weeks later and seemed to recover much better than we adults did. She went on to own other horses over the years. My heart, on the other hand, never got over that loss. There was no other single event in my life that I treated with more dignity, more community, or more honor than I did in the months that Ginger was in my barn.

If I had made up the story, I couldn't have written a more horrible ending than the one that actually happened. The only thing that could have possibly made that event worse was the fact that Frank, her beloved companion, died 30 days later. The vet claimed that he probably had a brain embolism, which was common in horses that had worked on the racetrack in their earlier years, but I believe he died of a broken heart.

I have yet to find any life lessons in Ginger's story. In all the years that I had worked with horses, I had never lost one, and within a span of 30 days, I said goodbye to two fine horses that had been someone else's throw-aways. My only desire was to care for them and find them good, loving homes, and they both died before that could happen.

Like the person who survives the tornado, but loses everything they own in the process, sometimes that's all there is. Sometimes surviving is as good as it gets. I left Whitehall within a few months of Ginger and Frank's deaths, because my heart just wasn't in it anymore. I no longer believed that if I cared enough, worked hard enough, and operated from the highest level of integrity that everything would work out just fine. I now know better….

Bonnie Marlewski-Probert

Biography: Bonnie Marlewski-Probert. Bonnie is a professionally trained horsewoman with 20 years of safe, responsible teaching and training experience. She has published more than 1000 magazine articles, several books and videos for horse lovers around the world. To learn more about Bonnie's work, visit her web site at TheCompletePet.com. To order books, call 800-700-5096 or order via the web site.

Jessie And The "City Slickers"

Many years ago, my older brother Peter invited me to join he and his two daughters Molly and Maren for a horseback ride at the local stable. The only time I had ever ridden was as a kid on a rental horse in Lake Tahoe. Peter, however, had always had a passion for horses and wanted one of his own. Inspite of my concerns about riding horses, it was important to accept the invitation. Not only because I love to spend time with my nieces, but for another reason.

You see, Peter had been diagnosed with cancer in 1992 at the age 33. Despite all the arguments of our childhood, Peter was facing the toughest battle of his life and I wanted to be there for him, so the four of us went for a ride.

What I didn't know until much later was that Peter secretly had his eye on a Buckskin mare at the barn that we were riding at that day. He wanted to buy the mare but couldn't afford her. In the tradition of all older brothers, Peter had set the whole thing up! He had brought the barn owner into his plan and it all hatched when we arrived at the barn that day. Coincidentally, "I" was given a beautiful Buckskin mare to ride for the day. We all had a wonderful time during that ride and upon our return, the barn owner took the time to mention that "I" was a natural on a horse.

The next thing I know she is telling me what a natural I am and that I should really think about riding. She would teach me, of course, and the horse we would use was the Buckskin. After the first lesson I am all stoked and my brother just happens to mention that the Buckskin is for sale. Well, we bought the horse and rode together all the time.

When we bought the mare her name was Jessie. We liked that name and decided to keep it. I will never forget the first time my brother and I rode together. We needed a second horse for our ride so we convinced the owner of our barn to let us use one of the horses from their rental string. Peter rode Jessie and I had the rental. We rode that day to a place called Ship's Mast, a large pine tree that resembled the mast of a ship. The whole way Peter was totally in charge, looking back to check on me and giving me tips on how to sit the horse. For a younger brother to take orders from his older brother is a difficult thing, but I didn't have a clue what I was doing and listened to everything he said. We had a great ride that day and I finally understood why Peter had such a passion for horses.

My brother and I had many more great rides including the time that Jessie bucked Peter off and came running back to the barn without him. From that day on we were forever known around the barn as the "City Slickers".

I never thought my brother and I would ever find a common thread, but we did in horses. He taught me everything and I listened and learned. He passed away not long after from the cancer, but I kept Jessie and have been passionate about horses ever since. I am not only grateful that Peter and I had the chance to spend that special time together before he passed away, but I am also grateful that he shared his passion for horses with this "City Slicker".

John Regin

Biography: John Regin. John works in San Francisco, California in the securities industry. He lives in Larkspur, just across the bay from San Francisco. "I grew up in this area, attended school Oregon and lived there until 1983 when I returned to California. I have worked as a volunteer for the Mounted Patrol Unit in the open space where I live, and this year started with the Marin County Sheriff's Posse. I own an eight-year-old Paint gelding named Chief and enjoy western pleasure riding in the area in which I live."

Chapter Eight
Gratitude

Rio's Babe

She came into our lives in 1986. We were looking for a quiet trail horse for my husband, Bob, and a friend mentioned that Babe was for sale. They had used her for trail riding and as a show horse for their children. I remembered seeing her on a video I had taken at our Judged Pleasure Ride. She was calmly walking along on a loose rein. We wanted to see more, so we went to look at her. At that time she was 14, a bay registered Quarter Horse with a blaze and a little snip on her coronary band. At 14.3 hands, she was the "old style" chunky (not to mention fat) Quarter Horse and we brought her home, not realizing how many years of pleasure she was to give us.

We all search for that perfect, "bomb-proof" horse, yet we all know there is no such thing as perfection. Babe was about as close as you could come. Bob had never ridden until he met me. He took up riding so we could spend more time together and I took up his sport of freshwater fishing. We often combined both by packing collapsible fishing poles in our saddlebags and riding to various streams to fish. The horses really enjoyed their rest while we were fishing.

Babe was the kind of horse that would take care of her rider. If she had a beginner in the saddle, she would plod along, never caring if she were first, last or in the middle of the pack. Yet when you asked her to do something, she was right there to do your bidding.

I remember once when a friend rode her, we wanted to practice our riding lessons and she asked her to do side passes, and turns on the forehand and hindquarters. Babe did them perfectly – even though she hadn't been asked to do that in years! You could put anyone up on her and they would always enjoy their ride. In fact, almost everyone who rode her offered to buy her. She was not for sale, a fact Bob had to tell people before they rode her. You could ride her alongside the road and she would not even flinch as a tractor-trailer went by. Out on the trail, she was the horse that would go through anything another horse might refuse to do; not blindly going through, but picking her way to make sure it was safe.

She got along well with other horses, and didn't have a lot of those annoying mare quirks. She had a wonderful disposition and endless patience, although she wasn't overly friendly. If you walked out into her pasture she wouldn't come to you, but you could walk up to her to pet or catch her. Of course, she would always come running at feeding time. That was another of her great qualities; she was an easy keeper. She stayed overly fat on a handful of grain. She loved to travel, and Bob always wished there was a contest for loading horses, because she would always win – if that trailer door was open, she was in it in a flash.

We rode her all over the New England states and she always settled in no matter where she was. Now, before you get to thinking that she was perfect, there was one thing she did that was annoying. Our horses have free access to the barn and pasture, but I swear she would leave the pasture to come into the barn to mess. My gelding, on the other hand, will not mess in his stall (unless he is locked in) and makes all his messes in certain spots in the pasture. She also had little tolerance for bugs, and would spent lots of time in the barn to get away from them. She would let you know they were annoying her by tossing her head while being ridden. Once you got rid of the pesky critters, she would stop the head-tossing.

As Bob's health deteriorated, he would ride less often, but no matter how long it was between rides, she would always be quiet and dependable for him. When Bob died in 1997, he left Babe to my five grandchildren, who live next door. They would come over to ride her in the ring, as they had done in the past, and she would patiently take all five of them around and around some more until they were all tired. Well, it may just have been Babe and Gramie who were tired – kids never seem to tire.

After Rachel, 11, had fallen off my horse, Babe was the one she rode to restore her confidence. Babe soon learned that Rebekah, 10, would allow her a few "shortcuts" and unplanned stops at the dismounting spot, while Nathan would insist she do what he asked. She would carry Rosharon, three, and Daniel, four, around while being led by one of the older siblings. She would patiently stand surrounded by kids while they groomed and fussed over her. Nathan, then nine, would come each day to help me feed, and he took over the barn cleaning chores. While he was shoveling, he would tell me he had the wrong horse and wondered if I wanted to switch. Sorry Nathan, even though that was a tempting offer, Gramie is smarter than that!

Despite Babe's age, her health remained good, except for heaves which were kept under control by limiting her access to hay. Her diet had been changed to a hay stretcher pellet, and a senior feed and a flake of hay to keep her occupied a little longer when there was no pasture to graze. At age 26, Babe developed Cushings Disease and she began to look like a teddy bear in the winter, with a long, thick, curly coat. She was slow shedding out in the spring, and her feet began to grow faster than normal.

Since her semi-retirement, Babe was accustomed to being left home while Leggs and I went off for a ride. She took this in stride and usually never acknowledged our comings and goings. One Saturday, however, she whinnied as we returned to the barn. I now wonder if she was saying hello or goodbye. That evening, she departed for the great pasture in the sky. She was buried in her pasture, where a stone with her name on it has been placed, and where we will plant a tree in her memory. We all miss her.

Aileen Livingston

Biography: Aileen Livingston. "I have spent many hours traveling with my 19-year-old Morgan gelding, Leggs, to pleasure trail ride and camp in many areas of the country. We have ridden in CT, NH, NY, MA, ME, RI, VT, PA, VA, and WV so far, and plan to go to Tennessee, Kentucky, Illinois and Ohio this year. Although all our trips have been wonderful, the most memorable was riding at Gettysburg. After each trip, I write about our adventures, and these articles have been published in *The Trail Rider* Magazine, and in the *Horsemen's Yankee Pedlar*. The story of our traveling companions, Bea and Chipper, was published in *Horse Tales for the Soul, Volume Two.*"

Gunner

I was actively competing in eventing at Training level, on my 19-year-old Thoroughbred gelding, Gunner. We seemed to be gone every other weekend. I loved to go to competitions with him. Then something happened that would change that forever.

It was Friday morning, the end of my spring break. I was planning on sleeping in, when my mom came into my room at 6:00 a.m. and woke me up. She said I needed to come to the barn to see my horse, because he was quivering. I really didn't think too much of it, and actually I was a little upset. I *really* wanted to sleep. I dragged myself out of bed, threw on some barn shoes, and went to see my horse.

It had gotten a little chilly that night, but not enough that he should have been shivering. We called the vet; my mom went to work, and I waited for him to come. Around 7:00 a.m. the vet arrived, and he treated Gunner for colic and took some blood to see if he was tying up. The tests came back negative, so we continued to treat him for colic. We kept a close eye on him; I slept out in the barn that night, and my mom took over for me in the early morning. We would walk him around every hour, and in the middle of the night, it was quite peaceful out there with him.

By Saturday, he seemed to be getting better, so we began to check on him every half hour. He hadn't been drinking, though, so he needed an IV to administer fluids into him. By Sunday night he seemed to be in pain, but he had finally begun to pass manure, so we thought that was why he was hurting. I slept in the barn that night, too.

By the early morning hours he was in severe pain, so my mom and I had to make a decision. We had said from the beginning that we didn't think surgery would be an option, because he was 19 years old and we could not really afford it. But when we were faced with the decision between surgery and putting him down, we had to take him to the clinic.

We loaded him into the trailer and began the hour-long trip to the clinic. On the way, I phoned my friend Martha to tell her about Gunner. I could barely get the words out of my mouth, so my mom had take the phone from me and explain the situation. Since Martha lived close to the clinic, she came to meet us there.

When we arrived, the vet examined Gunner. By this time, he was in so much discomfort that no matter how much painkiller he received, it wasn't helping. I was very relieved when he finally had anesthetic for surgery.

I watched the surgery with Martha and my mom. I was surprised at myself, because I tend to get queasy. I was doing all right until I saw the look on the doctor's face, which told me that it was over without even saying a word. I still did not believe it until I saw the large pink syringe. I recognized it from when we had to put down a horse at the barn that had a broken leg. By now I was screaming hysterically, and it echoed throughout the entire building.

After they cleaned him up, they let me in to say goodbye. With tears running down my face, I petted his velvet nose one last time. We then drove home, and talked and cried a lot. In a way, I was relieved that he was not in pain anymore. My mom and I talked about the many memories I have shared with my horse, all the good times and the bad.

It is now months later. I still miss him and I know I will for a long time. I never want to forget anything about him. I have a young horse right now that I am working with, and he is learning fast. I find myself comparing him to Gunner sometimes, which I know he will never be, but I'm glad I remember the way Gunner was. He will always be in my heart and I thank God for the six years I was able to spend with him.

Below is a poem I wrote the week after Gunner died:

You meant more to me than just any old horse,
You weren't just another mount on the cross-country course.
You were my friend and my partner, the one I did trust
To get me through that combination, where good striding's a must.

When I first started riding you, you scared me a lot,
You were in charge of our destination, more times than not.
As time went by, I learned to take control,
We then worked together to reach some new goals.

I planned a big year for us, I mapped it all out,
With many events and clinics, and PC Nationals no doubt.
But none of that matters, it's not important you see,
I just want to be with you, just you and me.

I miss your soft nose that nuzzled my back,
You always made me smile, you had quite the knack.
I miss you so much, I don't believe you are not here,
I feel kind of empty, inside I feel weird.

I've spent lots of time with you, several hours each day,
That time was so precious, you weren't in the way.
I just want to say thank you, thank you so much
For being a great teacher, you taught me a bunch.

I will never forget you as long as I live,
To you, a piece of my heart I will give!

I love you, Gunner!

Melissa Tonini

Biography: Melissa Tonini. "I am 19 years old and a current freshman at Stetson University. I started riding when I was 11 years old with my instructor, Bama Rogers. I learned solid basics from Bama, and she got me involved in the United States Pony club. I have been very involved in Pony Club for seven years, and sadly next year is my last one. I am currently working toward my HA and A ratings before I graduate. I am also a member of the United States Eventing Association. I am currently eventing a five year old that I am leasing. I keep my horse at my house (along with our two boarders), which is 10 minutes away from the university. My mom helps me out a lot in taking care of them. She has supported me for so long, and I want to thank her so much for it. I hope that there will always be horses involved in my life."

Trickster

One summer day, an older man was taking a walk when he happened to pass by where Trickster was grazing. "What a handsome old gentleman he is. I bet he has some good stories to tell about his younger days," the man said to me. So, I decided to tell some of the tales of our very special horse called Trickster.

It was in 1985 when I first met Trix at a lesson boarding barn where I had taken a job in New Hampshire. I was a city child who had finally made it to the country at the age of 32. Always loving horses, I didn't want to own one until I could care for it myself at my home.

Trix belonged to a boarder who took lessons on him and treated him kindly. She had bought him from a summer riding camp, because he was thin and overworked. He was a bright red 15-year-old chestnut gelding standing at about 15.3 hands. He had a habit of escaping from his turnout when he thought it was time to go in. He also opened his stall door unless it had a clip on the latch, and ran around the barn or arena creating lots of excitement. I enjoyed his clever escapes and started visiting him a lot.

My three-year-old son and four-year-old daughter, who accompanied me to work, liked to pet him and groom him. I noticed how gentle Trix was with them. He always made sure to stand very still when my children were with him. He loved the attention and care they gave him, so I offered to buy him if the owner ever wanted to let him go. Come the spring of 1985, she was moving, so using our tax refund, "The Trickster" became the family horse.

In the riding ring, with my son and daughter riding him, Trix was quiet, gentle and careful. His great love was to go out on the trails, which we explored for hours at a time in the back woods. His favorite time was when we would go racing with friends and their horses; his speed would even out - distance a long-legged Thoroughbred. Trix did flat work and jumping lessons with me for years with a willing disposition, but it wasn't his passion. His joy was to go out after lessons, even for a short trip, onto the trails.

After a year, we moved from the horse farm to our own home with a barn and then we bought a little palomino pony named Blaze to keep Trix company. Soon we bought a slightly larger pony, Matilda, to add to our herd.

Every spring, very early in the morning, Trix and I would go off by ourselves for a run to celebrate life. He would run until he could run no more and stand blowing, snorting, and prancing happily. Eventually Trix developed tendon problems and I used him only for trail riding. Some days when there wasn't time to ride, my husband and I would take the two ponies for walks like they were dogs. Trix especially enjoyed going to the lake to splash and roll in the water. We live way out in the woods, so when I went trail riding alone, I usually led a pony to help Trix be brave. We jokingly nick named Trix "strong heart" because of his fear of usually invisible terrors.

Often while cantering, I would find myself sitting on air when Trix did one of his famous leaps to the side to escape some imaginary monster. He would even remember where a deer or a dog had previously startled him and would still be on edge nearing that area, ready to save himself, even after months had passed.

Trickster was the first to greet me in the morning with his deep, soft nicker. No matter how quietly I tried to come into the barn, he would hear me and call out his greetings. When he was groomed, he would slowly fall asleep from total relaxation. He was the undisputed king of the ponies and with just a turn of his head and a fierce look, he would put any horse under his all-powerful rule.

As the years passed, he went into a gradual full retirement, but he never missed his early morning spring run. His teeth by this point were so worn down that he left hay balls everywhere because he couldn't chew properly. But, he enjoyed eating hay so much he was still given it and everyone joked about Trix's piles of hay balls. Eventually, his eyesight grew dim to that of a person in need of strong glasses. He was still happy with his small turnout and free access to a double stall. The three oldsters spent their days napping and grooming each other every day.

At the age of 33, his front tendons gave out on him. He kept re-straining them, because he would lay down a lot, and he would have to get himself up afterwards. Although comfortable on strong pain pills, I realized it was time to let my old friend go.

On a beautiful crisp sunny day in the fall, the time came. Trickster had enjoyed a peaceful day of eating, napping, and grooming his best pony pal, Blaze. I also groomed Trix and spent the day with him. Trix was put to rest as the sun was setting in a green rolling pasture at his home.

His mare, Tilly, called for him for three days and nights. Blaze mourns for his best friend still, but after nine months he is acting a little happier. Trickster taught everyone in the family many things and it was an honor to have had him in my life. I will miss him for the rest of my life, but picture him running strongly and happily in green pastures until we are all together again.

Elizabeth A. Berry

131

Biography: Elizabeth A. Berry. Born in Natick, Massachusetts, in 1953, Elizabeth was educated at the University of Massachusetts, with a degree in Park Administration. She moved to a small horse farm in Dublin, New Hampshire, with husband, Robert, son Jason and daughter Sarah. The dream of owning a horse was realized in 1985 with Trickster. The herd grew with Blaze of Lightning, Waltzing Matilda, Chesapeake Bay and Kelpie. Liz has learned much and been loved so well by many animal friends. She still resides in Dublin with horses and ponies, dogs Little Bear and Claw, cats Pearl and Skylar, and best friend, Bob.

Snowy Walk

It is one of those snowy days that occurs in all places that have wintry periods. The snow is falling in earnest, and we have been well warned of it since yesterday. The schools are either closed or out early. The grocery stores must surely be crowded. I-95 is a snarl with an 18-car pileup south of here in Ashland, Virginia, and the I-95/route 17 interchange is closed to traffic just down the road in Falmouth. CNN reports a 100-car back up on I-95 north of here, and Red Cross volunteers are taking travelers to shelters.

So, here we are, not really snowed in, but with no need to go out. However . . . out the kids go to do some barn work. Amanda has cleaned the stalls, and John brought in some sawdust and set up a small section of electric fence to keep Sam from chewing one of Mike's new trees.

I walk out to the barn and get Max's halter. This is really the first time it has snowed during our walks. The air is speckled with flakes that are falling rapidly. There is a satisfying crunchiness — almost a squeak – to the snow underfoot. I think a nice snowman or a snow fort could be built. Amanda and John talk of sledding once the barn work is finished. I walk out to bring Max in from the pasture. He is happy to see me, and with slicked-back evil-ears threatens the others for coming too close to his person.

He ducks his head into the halter and waits for me to fumble with big gloves on to fasten the buckle. We do our do-si-do through the gate and bid Mother Horse Penny and daughter Auntie April goodbye as we set out. Max is covered with snow sprinkles and has little ice drips in a line on his sides. His whiskers have a thin coating of ice from his warm breath. I knock out the snow and ice from his feet, scoop the snowflakes off his back, and we circle the riding ring to begin our walk.

The world is that quiet, muffled place that only happens during a real snow. No wind, just a drift of falling snow that stirs the air. Max is happy to be out and arches his neck and dances along, not impatient to be only walking, just happy to be alive, glad to be with a person, and interested in the scenery. He looks me full in the eye and we

132

know we are having fun. He snorts a couple of times and settles into the rhythm of the exercise. We climb a little hill and Cody Dog runs up behind us. Max snorts and dances, polite not to jerk the lead line. The lane is covered with fluffy snow, the birds are absent, hiding in the small cozy places in the brush.

At the bottom of the hill Max is ready to go, walking fast and effortlessly, me walking fast, taking short steps in the snow to make sure it is not slippery footing for a human. Max pulls on the lead rope, and jigs a little. I tell him to walk, he is eager and wants to go. We stride along the bottom near the little run, clear water running fast and silent. Cody Dog has deserted us.

Max is having fun, going on a tiny adventure in the snowy landscape. We pass the smooth silken water of the pond, and climb up the hill towards the house. Max is taking in the scenery, and sees Amanda and Arlo Pony at the top of the hill. He is eager to join them and jigs again, pulling the lead line. I tug the lead line and speak sternly to him; although he appears to ignore me, he settles and walks.

We are now into our second lap of the walk. We are neither cold nor hot, the exercise is enough to keep me warm, but not enough to make Max hot.

We can hear the muffled sound of a distant truck on the road, but the fearsome chickens are silent. All the other horses are eating freshly brought hay, but Max is glad to be out and about. Ears up, neck arched and head high, he swings along on our walk, watching the sights and reaching over to touch me with his muzzle now and then.

Soon our little walk is finished. We go into the barn to make sure no snow has balled up in his feet and to brush off the snow that has piled up on his back. Back to the pasture, a little do-si-do through the gate again, and Max waits politely to have his halter removed, standing quietly to be petted for a while, yawning and chewing happily. I step back outside the gate and latch it. Max, sniffing and pawing the snowy ground, finds a good place to roll, rises easily and shakes off the snow.

He puts on his slicked-back evil-ears and moves Auntie April from a hay pile that is especially tasty looking, wisely avoiding Mother Horse Penny: Queen of All She Surveys. As I return the halter to the barn, the three horses are peacefully munching their mid-morning hay. Snowflakes have begun to speckle Max's coat again.

Barbara Duell Hewitt

Biography: Barbara Duell Hewitt. "I have always loved horses and for most of the last 35 years I have been privileged to share my life with horses and ponies. My family and I have a small farm near historic Fredericksburg, Virginia, where we enjoy the many pleasures of horsekeeping."

The Sweetest Ride

We were wrapping up a clinic in Texas. We did a few days worth of bodywork, groundwork and lessons. The weather was crisp, as the day before we worked horses in the wide-open pasture, buffeting winds from the passing storm. Aside from freezing our buns off, everyone seemed to get a great deal out of the work we did.

I was to catch my plane home that afternoon, but squeezed in one more session with my host. We had been building a relationship for a while now. Using animal communication, she "heard" what her horse was going through, through his point of view. The initial consultations told us the horse, a barrel racer, was experiencing pain in his hip.

It has been several years now. With the help of a holistic vet, Reiki and bodywork which the owner learned, as well as educating herself in proper riding (bending energy) and not just imposing her will on the horse, it all culminated in a horse that was a willing partner and not a machine taking orders.

After fine-tuning some groundwork, the owner hopped on. She showed me how her horse and she have come together under saddle since the last time I was there. They had definitely progressed. She rode up and asked me to give him a ride. I climbed aboard. I started to walk him around the pasture. It had rained heavily the night before, so the ground was saturated. Many people worry about footing after such a storm and rightly so. However, once you really learn to bend energy, as I like to call it, you can literally ride each foot down into the ground with security.

The quality of his footsteps told me he was ready to transition up to a faster gait. I raised my energy level and barely squeezed with my calves. He responded with a wonderfully light trot. His mouth gently asked for more; I basically just thought "canter" and off he went. Under the wide-open Texas sky in the brisk morning air he was ready to go off to the races. I could feel that big body really wanting to go through his paces, but I had different paces in mind.

A few romps around the pasture later, I felt him ready to go to work. I sucked my energy up and back with every stride. He responded by raising his back. I could feel every vertebra in his back soft and loose. This made his legs and feet swing freely from that beautiful bay body of his. He rounded up and was the pinnacle of self-carriage in that pasture. The reins were loose and he was working strictly off intent. There was no pulling, no excessive leg, just bending energy at its finest. I would suck my energy back and think "trot" and down he would transition into a wonderfully engaged trot – the kind that says, "my back doesn't hurt anymore!" With a slight raise in my own energy, he was off in the canter. Changing direction, transitions, no problem! Easy as pie. I could think our next move, adjust my energy and it would come about.

And there under that big open Texas sky, everything in the world was right. Everything I had experienced in life came together to teach me what life was all about and to do the work I was intended to do here on earth. I swear that day; I could feel God smile in the winter sunshine! It moved me to tears that such a large and wonderful beast could be as one with me and work off shear intent. The world could have started or ended that day and it wouldn't have mattered to me. I was the luckiest person on earth to have the ability to do the work I love and to do it well. My life had purpose and meaning and I could pass that blessing on to others. How fortunate I am. I rode to the far side of the pasture to compose myself, as I was a bit overcome.

When I rode back to the owner, I saw she too was teary-eyed. I asked her why. She said that was one of the most beautiful rides she had witnessed. I, too, had to share my moment with her.

I have the good fortune of finding a moment like this every day, may you do the same!

Renate Andrasevits

Biography: Renate Andrasevits. Renate has more than 20 years of experience rehabilitating problem horses. Her work has been covered in Natural Horse Magazine and on the popular Animal Planet television network. Her methods include incorporating animal communication along with "bending energy", so riders can achieve harmony with their horses. She also specializes in energywork, bodywork, Equine Touch, Bioscan and herbal therapies to rehabilitate all animals. Renate offers Lessons and clinics which are available for animal communication, bodywork, groundwork and riding. Consultations can be scheduled by phoning Renate at 310-782-1863, via e-mail at generen2@netscape.net or by writing to her at: Windwalker Animal Communication and Rehabilitation 1446 W. 216th Street, Torrance, CA 90501.

His Spirit Roams In Our Hearts Forever

Author's note: Although I wrote the following words about Tristan, I refer to myself in the third person. I am a mere instrument for the collective of children who rode and loved this extraordinary horse over the final five years of his existence. Just as I was blessed with his exquisite spirit when I taught with him, may I now be graced with the words to express and honor the vast worth of his life.

Anyone with money can find a flashy horse to buy. But a horse that shines from the inside out is another matter.

135

That is what Tristan came to do after coming to Wildfire Farm Children's Center in the spring of 1996. What a mess he was on his arrival: underweight, mentally confused, depressed and spiritually alienated. Because of chronic massive diarrhea, he had been kicked out of the barn where he had been leased as a school horse and he wasn't welcome anywhere else. Judy agreed to give him a free stall in exchange for permission to try to rehabilitate him and use him in her children's therapeutic riding program when she felt he was ready.

A holistic animal communicator and healer as well as an instructor, Judy designed a healing program that included not only proper care on a physical level, but also Reiki sessions, counseling and unconditional love from her and the children on a psycho-spiritual level. She intuitively knew that his diarrhea was a symptom of the anger that had gathered in him from his long, hard life and that it could be healed by assigning him a role as "wise elder and keeper of the children."

Tristan (who in one version of Arthurian legend was the noblest of knights) rose to the occasion. Within ten days of his arrival, children in the after-school program were riding him bareback, feeling safe and at home as a result of his broad back and quiet, loving manner. The episodes of diarrhea became less and less frequent and soon stopped completely. His body became plump and muscled, and his dull chestnut coat was transformed to glistening mahogany. He broadened his capabilities from Western pleasure to first level dressage and up to two-foot jumps, showing exceptional willingness and patience with children of all ages. He came to excel as a special needs children's horse, and in less than two years after coming to us was receiving major notice in the press.

Two months after Tristan's arrival, Judy was able to buy him for only $600. After his rehabilitation, Judy's riding instructor offered to buy him for a great deal more than that amount despite his lack of papers and his advanced years (he was at least in his mid-twenties). But he was not for sale at any price, and would spend the rest of his days in his new home with his beloved children.

He became famous for making people feel safe and empowered, and an average of 30 children and teenagers per week flourished in the presence of his unconditional love. These riders included not only mainstream kids with the stress and troubles of everyday life, but also at-risk teenagers and kids of all ages with special challenges such as autism, ADD/ADHD, attachment disorder, depression, anxiety and recovery from neglect and abuse. Judy has videotapes of Tristan teaching a boy who had suffered enormous abuse; the stunning progress of this child over time testifies to the power of Tristan's bottomless patience and love. As we look back over the lives that Tristan touched, we find his betterment of our world to be staggering.

For several months before he died, everyone noticed that Tristan was especially joyful, even coming up with new tricks such as tossing rubber training cones around and going down on his knee while playing with Wildfire's new Premarin rescue colt (Tristan had a nose for others who had suffered in life and was quick to offer compassion and solace). Everyone at Wildfire is convinced that Tristan's increased joy near the end of his life was caused by his awareness that his time with us was coming to an end and that he had lived the last five years of his life so well, so nobly. The kids and Judy talked about that a lot, about what it must mean to be able to die with such peace of mind, and that made his passing easier to bear.

Of all the lessons that he taught us – about turning personal suffering into service, about looking beyond the external to the great heart that lies within, about day in and day out loving kindness – the lessons we learned from his passing mean the most. We learned that a life well lived is a reason for joy, and our end of the year after-school riding show was dedicated to Tristan as a celebration of his time with us. We learned that we reap what we sow, and were not surprised at the throngs of people who came to say goodbye. We learned that he didn't really leave us; one child wrote that his spirit roams in our hearts forever, another that we should not stand at his grave and cry, for he is a pure spirit which did not die.

Tristan surely did not leave us the same as he found us; after knowing him, we became both larger and deeper than we had been before. One 11-year-old girl who is in the foster care system after suffering the worst of abuse put it this way in her tribute to Tristan's memory:

> I looked at a fox; I heard her spirit sing,
> I opened my heart and listened, for ears hear not a thing,
> It was then I finally realized - why did this take so long?
> You see, my friend and I were singing the very same song.

Good for you, Tristan, good for you!

Judith H. Young, Ph.D.

Biography: Judith H. Young, Ph.D., Reiki Master, is Executive Director of Wildfire Farm Holistic Children's Services, 103 Kensington Road, Hampton Falls, NH 03844. Wildfire is a nonprofit organization dedicated to promoting the healthy development of children through animal and nature therapy, which is provided by horses and other farm animals. Judy is also a hands-on healer and animal intutitive; she offers sessions for people and animals as well as classes and certification in Reiki and in holistic animal communication and healing. She can be reached at 603-926-7476 or wildfirefarm@yahoo.com. Wildfire Farm's web site is http://geocities.com/wildfirefarm.

Whizteria - A Silver Lining

The little filly touched my heartstrings the day she was born. I had only recently re-entered the world of horses after raising a family and establishing a career for myself after my children were grown.

The first horse I owned as an adult was Lilli, a bay half-Arabian mare. With the purchase came 60 days' training with a trainer who lived near me in North Carolina. I had been working with the trainer for several weeks when I arrived just in time one Sunday morning. Her Arabian broodmare had just given birth to a beautiful gray filly and the imprint process was about to begin.

Like a magnet, I was drawn to the birthing stall where the trainer and her teenaged daughter were touching and rubbing the filly all over her body, taking great care to tap tiny hooves, touch eyes, ears, nose and mouth until the sensation was completely second nature to her. Then they took plastic and crackled it over the filly's body, ran clippers without blades over her body and sprayed water from a bottle to simulate fly spray. This was repeated two more times during the day.

The trainer explained that the goal of this technique is to get the foal's comfort level with humans to a point where it is accepting of touching and commands from the humans. I was very impressed with the whole concept and was determined to learn more. I went home and ordered the video of Dr. Robert Miller's "Early Learning", which details his method of imprint training the foal.

The little gray filly was named Whizteria, after her famous sire, SHF Southern Whiz. Each weekend for four months, I observed Whizteria while trying to concentrate on working with Lilli and the trainer. Then I made a life-changing decision.

I had decided to move to Tennessee and planned to purchase a farm there with my husband. In addition to giving up my career and my North Carolina roots, that meant giving up the Sundays I had grown so accustomed to, what I fondly called "Whizteria watching".

In the meantime, the trainer had sold me a beautiful black Arabian mare, Auja Maria, who was a pleasure to ride. Lilli had been bred and was now in foal and we would have our own baby next April. But as I made plans to move to Tennessee, Whizteria was on my mind.

At this point in my life, I had virtually no experience with horses as an adult, so two horses, one of which was in foal, and a totally new lifestyle on a farm with my husband were enough for me to handle. Still, I wished I could have taken Whizteria with me.

In April, Lilli delivered a beautiful bay filly of her own and we named her Diamahn 'Lil. I took so much pleasure in the everyday care of this tiny baby and she was a delight. Life went on and was very busy for me, with each day bringing new challenges.

I made two trips a year back to the trainer's barn for what we called "refresher courses" in riding and training, but also to visit and catch up. Part of my visit was aimed at seeing for myself how Whizteria was growing. Back home again, I fretted over her so much that when the weather was very cold and icy I would call the trainer to make certain that Whizteria was warm and dry. The trainer kept Whizteria in the pasture except for bad weather days, but she was much happier outside and didn't care for stall living at all.

When Whizteria was two years old, I purchased a gray broodmare and decided to breed her to the trainer's stallion. Auja Maria had been given a breeding as part of the purchase two years ago, so I decided to send both horses to the trainer's that spring. Both horses came into season and were bred. When the gray mare was 30 days in foal, she developed a sudden bout with colic. She had an impassable impact and had to be put down. We were devastated. I grieved for the mare, but I grieved even more for the tiny life that was lost.

Soon after the gray mare died, the trainer called to ask me if I was thinking at all about another gray mare. I told her that it was too soon. She said when I was ready, she wanted to send me a video of Whizteria in motion. Now she really had my attention. Certain that Whizteria, the most beautiful of fillies, would have a price tag I could not afford, I told her to go ahead and send it. What was the harm in looking?

When the tape arrived I ran to the house and watched it with tears streaming down my face. This little filly that I had first seen on the morning she was born had grown into a gorgeous rose gray beauty. She seemed to float as she walked, trotted and cantered around the trainer's arena. As taken aback as I was, I knew that this horse was being marketed big time, nationally and internationally.

Whizteria's sister, SHF Pearlie Mae, was 1996 World Champion Mare in halter and lives in England. So, it made sense to the trainer to place her in the world market. Whizteria was definitely out of my league. But for the past two years I had asked after her with each conversation, wanting to make sure that if she were sold I knew where she went. I definitely wanted to keep tabs on this horse and follow her successes.

One day in mid-January, 1999, the trainer called and said that she had been thinking about Whizteria and me and that we should talk. I was very receptive and listened to her explain about the appraisal on Whizteria, of the interest in her from different areas of the country, and about her desire to place her with someone who would love her and give her the best possible life. "That's me," I thought to myself, "That's me." I told her that while I would dearly love to have Whizteria, I knew I couldn't afford her. She said that we should both think about what we could do monetarily and talk again soon.

I tried to busy myself with other things so that I wouldn't even think of attempting to buy Whizteria. We had incurred a lot of vet bills over the past year and we still needed to make some improvements to the farm. We couldn't take money from the budget to purchase another horse, even if that horse was Whizteria, the horse of my dreams. I busied myself with projects around the farm and tried not to dwell on the impossible.

Then one day about two weeks later, the trainer left a message for me and I returned the call. She outlined what was a truly remarkable deal, especially since I knew what Whizteria was worth on the market. She really wanted me to have that horse and had gone to great lengths to make me an offer that she thought I couldn't refuse. But while mentally calculating, I just thought out loud and said, "It's a shame you don't like jewelry." "What kind of jewelry?" she asked. I went on to explain that I had a wedding ring that had been custom made for me and that I no longer had a need for it. In fact, I very seldom wore it at all. I told her that I had a written appraisal for more than she was asking for Whizteria, but on the market the ring would probably not bring as much as the appraisal. "I can't even think of taking your wedding ring," she said. "Why not? A ring can't nuzzle you and give you horse kisses," I replied. "I'd much rather have a horse than a ring." To my surprise, the trainer said that she did like jewelry and that she would think this over and see if she could justify the trade. I didn't even consider the possibility that she would say yes.

The next day, the trainer called and said that she was in the mood to make a deal. Today was to be my lucky day. Whizteria was mine! The trainer asked me to place insurance on Whizteria and call her back. When this was done, she would take the registration papers to the post office and send them to me. The deal was made!

With the trade, the trainer gave me 60 days' training for Whizteria and she was started three months before her third birthday. On April 1, I drove to the trainer's barn and we began our training together. She was so beautiful, I couldn't believe that this horse was mine. I worked with her for a week, then the trainer and her mother followed me back to Tennessee with Whizteria.

140

When I look back over the last three years, it's clear that Whizteria was on my mind much of the time. It was as though a plan was put into motion the day she was born. I'm so glad that plan included me, because the trainer could have easily sold her to someone else. She made a big sacrifice in order for me to have Whizteria and I will be eternally grateful to her for that. But she could not have chosen a place where Whizteria would have been loved more. In fact, the morning the trainer left to go home, I silently crept into the barn to see the two sharing one last hug. The trainer told Whizteria, "You be a good girl, Whizteria. You'll have a good home with lots of love." Truer words cannot be spoken because Whizteria makes it so easy for me to love her. She is indeed my silver lining.

Emily Lineberger Bridges

Biography: Emily Lineberger Bridges. A North Carolina native, Emily Lineberger Bridges was involved with horses as a child. With adulthood came other responsibilities, but she dreamed of the day when horses could take priority. In 1992, Emily began riding again, and in 1996 she moved with her Arabian horses to Lebanon, Tennessee. With this move came a start-up horsekeeping operation, including a family-built barn. She and her husband, Ron, own Summerwind Farm where they raise purebred and half-Arabian horses with Polish and Crabbet bloodlines. Their primary focus is on breeding and foal development. Emily's description of her life with her horses? "Living the Dream!"

In an upcoming book entitled "Dear Dolly", Emily shares her life-changing experiences with horses. Complete with tips for horse owners, the book is entertaining and educational. It can be ordered by calling 1-800-700-5096 or online at http://TheCompletePet.com.

Horse Fear, A Father's Love

My left knee was bloody from my horse slamming me into a tree along the path and now we were running in an open field. I held on tightly, but a quick stop and a lowered head sent me flying over the front of the horse. I was nine years old and attending a church summer camp. I vowed to never ride a horse again and managed to keep that promise for more than 35 years.

In the summer of 2001, a friend brought a few ponies for the children to ride during a church picnic. My youngest child, seven-year-old Lisa, beamed as she sat on the pony while being led around a short path. She rode three times. Lisa likes all animals, so I thought little of the event. On her next trip to the toy store, Lisa brought home a toy horse and slept with it – but she usually sleeps with every new toy she purchases. The next month, the fair was in town and she found the pony ride. After this, Breyer ponies began to arrive at the house.

I set my own fear aside long enough to search for a good riding school. After all, I reasoned, it was not as if I had to ride the horse myself – thank goodness! I knew of a horse supply store (I think I'm supposed to call them "tack stores") on the other side of town. The owner provided me with a list of 20 stables within a 50-mile radius that give lessons. Of course, I checked out the closest one first.

I took Lisa with me, since we like adventures. The first facility had an old Chevrolet's seat sitting out front of a rundown barn. The horses were running loose everywhere, having apparently escaped through one of many broken sections of fence. The owner/trainer was having a loud argument with one of her children. We left quietly.

The second place was beautiful and prompted other positive first impressions. The trainer showed us the facilities and I explained that Lisa needed to learn how to ride properly as well as care for the horse. She is my princess, but I am trying to raise a reasonable young lady here. The trainer informed me that "the children" were not allowed in the barn. The horse would be brought to Lisa in the riding ring. By this time, I thought I might have to visit all 20 barns on my list. I felt a little like Goldilocks in the story of The Three Bears.

The third place had a lot of cars parked in the front lot. I took this as an encouraging sign; you know, sort of like how you pick a restaurant when you're out of town. You look for the ones that are crowded, because you have better odds of getting a good meal. There were a number of parents and kids everywhere smiling and laughing. After we toured the facility I learned that the very next Saturday they were beginning an introductory course for kids. This felt "just right." I signed Lisa up.

The group lessons went well. In just a few weeks Lisa was taking private lessons. She quickly learned to post while trotting and to canter. It wasn't long before Lisa and her mother, who rides, were planning a spring horse riding vacation. I had never shared my history or fear of horses with my wife, Cindy. I have always been reasonably athletic over the years, so I guess she just assumed I could ride. Cindy had no clue that she and Lisa would be riding off into the sunset without me. Well, what kind of father was I?

The next day, I called Lisa's riding teacher and made an appointment for my first lesson. The big day arrived: Lisa and I had back-to-back lessons. I knew that if she attended it would hard for me to be able to back out. I was given the owner's horse to ride … and it was a monster! He was so big that I could not get my foot into the stirrup. Of course, being middle-aged, inflexible and 25 pounds overweight had nothing to do with it. I looked at Lisa and she was grinning at me as I mounted the horse by climbing up the steps little kids use to get on their horses. Off to a good start!

I was a little uncomfortable as the teacher led me around in a circle on what she called "a lunge line." It got worse, as I had to pretend I was an airplane. The theory here was I was learning how to balance on the horse. I think my young teacher just really enjoyed watching a short, middle-aged, overweight man trying to be *Joe Cool* while being an airplane on a horse. As my teacher patiently taught me to ride, step-by-step, my confidence began to grow.

I graduated from the lunge line to actually guiding the horse. I learned to trot in circles. It was nice that the horse actually let me think I was steering him. It did not seem long before the hour was over. Not only had I finished the lesson, but I also enjoyed myself. As I got off the horse I misjudged how far I was from the ground. This resulted in a sudden and unexpected appearance of the ground close to my face. I truly understood how Charlie Brown must feel when Lucy pulls the football away as he tries to kick it.

As I rose to me feet I felt pain in my legs, which had been reluctantly forced into a strange position for the first time. Feeling a little triumphant in just completing the lesson, I was surprised when my teacher laughed and told Lisa, "Your daddy is a wimp." I was embarrassed and wondered what has happened to me over the years. I may not have excelled at sports, but I did compete as a young man in high school in wrestling, track and tennis.

Heels down, knees bent, straight back, belly out, head up, arms down in line with the horse's bit, and – of course, my favorite – thumbs up. What does that do? I must confess it is a little like taking golf lessons. They put your body in unnatural positions and then say, "Hit the ball." Well, with horses they put your body in line (yeah, right) and then say, "Now, ride."

As we drove home, and throughout the following evening, Lisa told the story of Daddy's first lesson to anyone who would listen. However, I thought it went much better than she described. But she did say, "Daddy can do it, if he really tries."

Who's the parent here, anyway?

Edward "Lee" Bell

Biography: Edward "Lee" Bell. Lee is married for ten wonderful years to a beautiful and loving wife Cindy. He is a short, slightly overweight (well possibly a little over slightly) middle-aged father of three who lives and rides (yeah, right) in Knoxville, Tennessee. In his spare time, Lee searches the Internet for family riding vacations and scans local newspapers for property on which to build a small stable and new home. He has volunteered to help a friend from church - the one who brought ponies to the picnic and started this process - build a new barn in the spring. Lee's horse fear has transformed into horse fever. He spends most of his time trying to love his children and friends in the way his Heavenly Father taught him.

Chapter Nine
Junior Horse Tales

Redneck Pony

When my daughter, Casey, was eight years old, we bought her a small Appaloosa pony named Ariel. She was very honest and taught Casey many lessons, along with instructions in the art of riding. Two years later, when Casey began to outgrow Ariel, we bought her son Magic Man, a five-year-old Paint pony we knew to have Ariel's disposition, even though he did not have her experience. Such began our journey with our redneck pony.

The people we purchased Magic from told us that when Magic was born, Ariel had him right in the midst of a patch of ferns. When they found him they knew it was Magic. Little did we know how Magical this pony would be in Casey's life.

Casey had outgrown Ariel in size, but not in heart. She was having a hard time moving up to her larger pony, as he did not have as much experience and the pair would have to work harder. Casey was always one to do just enough to get by. Magic, it seemed, had a personality much like Casey's – he just wanted to do *just enough* to get by. When Casey and Magic practiced, it was obvious that Magic was much more interested in the next carrot coming his way, for his next scratch on the forehead, or what was going on in the field next door. He would untie himself just to let us know he could, because he never went anywhere.

When standing waiting for Casey to mount or after being ridden, his stature was very lazy, feet spread apart, never giving a hoot how he looked, thus I dubbed him our "redneck pony". Magic was also very loudly marked in color. People would laugh when I called him a redneck, but after being around him for a while they certainly understood where I was coming from. Magic's disposition was great and when Ariel was pregnant and Casey was forced to ride Magic, the bond began to strengthen. I finally had to keep my "redneck pony" comments to myself, because my daughter would get highly upset with the thought her pony was not perfect.

My two daughters had always been in 4-H and competed in local shows, ultimately to go to the 4-H state competition at the end of the year. I was worried this year, because Casey had taken Ariel to the state competition last year and won a championship in her division of Pony Western Pleasure. I was afraid my daughter had not yet learned how to accept the agony of defeat. I have always tried to teach them that winning is a bonus; the enjoyment of the competition and the companionship of your friends and horses is truly what is important. I was still afraid she would have her feelings hurt when she didn't win and tried to prepare her, as Magic was still green in his training and Casey was doing all the training herself.

The summer went on and we took Magic to several local horse shows. Casey and Magic would occasionally win a ribbon and they were having fun. Magic still didn't seem to get it. He just didn't care about getting that proud look and trying to be a show pony. He would do just enough to get by and so would Casey. How could I prepare them for state competition without discouraging them?

Casey kept on with Magic's training without the aid of an instructor, as her instructor was going back to school and we still hadn't found someone to replace her. Casey was determined to take her redneck pony to the state fair.

The week finally came and we headed for the beautiful Virginia Horse Center to compete. The drive was a couple of hours and we knew we would be at the horse center the day before competition, so we decided to wait to bathe the ponies upon arrival after they had the chance to settle in. On the drive to the show, I tried to gently prepare Casey, saying that she probably would not win anything as state competition was tough and Magic was green. It was important that she go to have a good time.

Magic was put into his temporary stall and he acted like his redneck self. He screamed and screamed at all the horses and I was beginning to worry if this had indeed been a mistake to bring him. Maybe he wasn't ready for this kind of competition. We took our time with him and showed him his stable mate was in the stall beside him. He finally settled down. Many of the other kids came over to see the dirty Paint pony.

We took Magic out of his stall to groom him before his bath. He had settled down all right. There he stood with feet spread apart, his redneck self. I was a little embarrassed. All the other kids have regal horses cleaned to perfection and seeming to stand proudly, knowing they were there to show their best. Magic took it all in while we were grooming him. He stood very quietly, looking around. We took him to the wash stall and cleaned him from top to bottom and when Magic came out it was like a transformation. He stepped out of that wash stall with head held high, with all the regal glory of a prince. I thought I was just imagining this, but others also seemed to notice. The 4-H leader even made a comment about how beautiful he looked and Casey was very proud. I finally realized the Casey was proud of Magic for what he was. It didn't matter about the ribbons he won. He took care of her and they loved each other. Most of all, they accepted each other for what they were. It seemed I was the one to learn a lesson from this competition. I was always trying to push Casey to give 102%. I finally learned she just needed to be herself.

Casey and Magic competed in several classes that week, and they placed in every class except one. They didn't win first place and it didn't matter. They both gave just enough to make each other proud and it came from the heart. At the next 4-H meeting, the leader announced a special recognition to Casey and her pony for the ability to go to such a large competition with such little experience and give it all they had with such an outstanding attitude.

Casey and Magic are still competing in local and state horse shows occasionally. Neither one of them are interested in being on any Olympic team. They are still just having fun giving just enough. They take care of each other and share a special bond. I'm less stressed these days. I stopped pushing and am enjoying watching my daughter just be herself. She's going to be fine. Oh, and Magic is not our redneck pony anymore. He's our Magic Man.

Mitzi Santana

Biography: Mitzi Santana. Mitzi and her daughters, Ashley and Casey reside in the beautiful state of Virginia. Mitzi was raised around horses, riding before she could walk. Since then, she has enjoyed many disciplines in riding but admits her favorite is a trail ride with her family. She is an active 4-H volunteer for the Horse N Around Fluvanna 4-H.

All Horses Have A Heart

Ever since second grade, I loved horses. I wrote stories and poems about these beautiful creatures, and was interested in everything about them. I started riding in fourth grade and a few years later I went to a camp in Pennsylvania which offered a centered riding program called ranch camp. The barn had about 20 horses that the camp rented from local people for the summer. Lots of the horses were disobedient or had stable vices, but the camp could rent them for a low price.

When I went to camp that year, my class had just started to canter. I wasn't at all steady with the canter and didn't know right from wrong with leads. I was good at trotting, walking, jumping, and even acquired a strong leg. I thought I would be ready for this class.

It was my fourth or fifth day at ranch camp. I looked at the board to see who each of us was riding. David - Apachee, Carly - Sienna, Perry - Duncan, and Kristen - Sid. I was riding Sid. Sid was a light bay Quarter Horse with pretty good manners. We brought out our horses and tied them to the outside riding ring. Then I went back for my grooming kit. The four of us had learned how to groom horses a few days ago. I went back into the barn after I was done grooming Sid and got his saddle and bridle. Ugh, I was riding Western today. I liked English so much better. I tacked him up and I have to admit, I had a hard time getting the bit in his mouth.

147

The four of us mounted and began walking the three horses, Sid, Duncan, Sienna, and the little pony, Apachee, to warm them up. First we worked on our position, halting, and reversing. Then we worked on our two-point trot, posting trot, and sitting trot. Next, Sandy, our riding instructor, said we were going to canter. First Carly went, but she could not get Sienna to canter for her, since he's a very lazy horse. Sandy instructed Perry just to trot, because he was not that experienced. Next came my turn.

I got Sid trotting easily. We were doing fine until I clapped my outside leg on him to get him cantering. Instead of cantering, he started trotting as fast as a racing trotter! We were flying down the side of the ring and I lost control. I could not steer. I just kept thinking that he was not going to round the corner, but go straight and jump over the fence surrounding the ring. Clop, clop, clop, clop. Faster and faster Sid trotted, when to my relief at the end of the ring he jerked to the side and continued around. I pulled myself together and concentrated on halting him. I had my legs glued to his side, not to make him go faster, but for fear of losing balance. But Sid was confused, for as my legs were speeding him on, I was pulling back on the reins.

I was in for something big! Sid didn't know what I wanted him to do, so he bucked powerfully in the air and I held on for my life. As soon as he came down from the buck he reared. I slid right off his back, directly behind his back legs, and frantically scooted to the side so I wouldn't get kicked. I sat there dazed, watching him whinny and trot in a small circle, wondering what he would do next. Finally, he slowed down in front of me, then leaned his head in and nuzzled me. I think he wanted to know if I was all right. He was nudging my side for me to get up.

Luckily, I was stunned but not hurt. Aside from a weird feeling in my left wrist, I was okay. Sid's head was by my side, encouraging me to get up. I gave him a pat and told him everything was all right, and stood up. Sandy asked if I was okay and then asked if I wanted to try to canter again. This time, we went down the side and I gave him a squeeze with my outside leg and we cantered nicely.

Even though I was still a beginner, I learned a lot that day. I realize that the horse depends on my signals and body language to guide him. Although the horse and rider appear as one, the horse is, after all, a beast, while the rider is an intellectual being. But it seemed that day that Sid had just as much compassion and caring as any human. Before this, whenever I looked into a horse's eyes, I only suspected that these magical creatures had the capacity of kindness. Now I know with certainty, all horses have a heart.

Kristen Brooks

Biography: Kristen Brooks. Kristen Brooks is a 13-year-old girl who lives in central New Jersey. She is interested in show jumping and dressage, and has been riding for five years. She hopes eventually to pursue equine studies in college and have a career that keeps her around horses.

A Special Gift

Drs. Donald and Debra Pepper kindly donated 18 American Saddlebred horses from their farm to our 4-H club. Dr. Debra Pepper was sadly diagnosed with terminal cancer and it was her wish that these horses would go to the children of our club. She knew through the 4-H program that these kids would be overseen to get a good education on how to care for their animals and that these horses were going to kids who would not otherwise have had the chance to own a horse of their own. Her horses' welfare was more important than money. It gave her "peace of mind" knowing her horses were going to loving homes. She sadly died shortly after our club received this generous gift.

After all the horses arrived at the club, we were taught how to care for them. Our leader taught us how to feed, groom, halter and lead our horses. We were taught the parts of the saddle, bridle and horse. The horses stayed there until we felt confident enough to care for them ourselves and take them home.

While the horses were at the farm, we had a horse show. There was no riding in our show, however. We had classes such as who could groom their horse the best in 15 minutes, who could saddle and bridle their horse in the fastest time, and guess the height of a horse. Other events were naming five parts of the saddle, five parts of the bridle and five parts of a horse. We had to lead our horse around an obstacle course in the shortest amount of time, too. All the events were topics that our leader had taught us in as a part of the preparation for us to take our horses home.

This was my first horse show and Supremacy and I won! After that first show, I knew I was really hooked on horses. It was then I also decided that one day I would work with horses for a living.

In her honor, our club has a Dr. Debra Pepper Memorial High Point Trophy at our farm show. Last year Manhattan Supremacy and I won the trophy. I can't explain to you how honored I felt to receive it. Later that year, together we won the American Saddlebred Pleasure Championship at the State Fair.

I am so privileged and humbled to have one of those Saddlebreds today. I think of Dr. Debra Pepper every time I ride my horse and one day, I hope to be able to give another child the same opportunity that she gave me. I thank her from the bottom of my heart!

Kendall Whitt

Biography: Kendall Whitt. "I am a 16-year-old sophomore at Culpeper County High School and the youngest girl of four children. For eight years, I have played softball in our county little league and I am very active in 4-H and my school's Future Farmers of America (FFA) Chapter.

I did not get involved with horses until I was 11, and they have truly become my passion. I own an American Saddlebred and compete in Saddle Seat shows. The award I am most proud of winning is the American Saddlebred Pleasure Championship at the Virginia State Fair. I also compete in Horse Judging and Hippology contests. Recently, I received a Paint filly to train as part of a 4-H project. I hope to one day become a respected horse trainer and until then, I will be as involved as I can with horses."

Visit To Commodore Oliver Hazard Perry Homestead

The day started out just right – the weather was fine, all the horses were fed, stalls were cleaned and bedded down and the children were off to their first day of school on time. But everything changed when the police called to say that our horses were seen running down the busy highway. They were seen by another caller who said they were turning into the lane leading to the historical birthplace and homestead of Commodore Oliver Hazard Perry.

Here I was with four horses out, children in school, and my husband could not be reached. I would have to find help somewhere. The first thing I had to do was make a list of items to bring with me to lead them back home. I kept telling myself *don't panic, it's going to be okay, yes, I can do it.*

Another call came saying the horses were all on the front lawn, eating away on the lush green grass. The owner of the property would keep the horses there until help arrived to lead them back to their barn. If they tried to shoo the horses away, they thought they would go back out onto the highway and there was no telling what might happen to four loose horses.

I managed to get some help from a few neighbors familiar with horses and soon the children arrived home from school, being excused for "dangerous" reasons.

I drove my car, loaded with helpers and items I needed. I parked my car sideways in the lane, blocking the horses in should they run from us. I think they were glad to see us, because of the cooperative way they let us put their halters and lead ropes on. As we walked along the highway leading the horses, it started to rain, which added to our problems. As the traffic became busy, we had several "smart Alec" drivers holler out, "Why don't you get on the horses and ride them?" But no one rides horses on that busy highway, especially without saddles.

When we got back to the farm, we discovered that the man who had been working on the new stretch of road dividing our farm into two parts had taken several sections of fencing down and the horses just walked out and down the road. To add a little humor to this wild event, I told the children that Mary had a little lamb that followed her to school one day, and the horses wanted to do the same thing, but just lost their way.

The response from one child: "Yeah mom, always an excuse."

Alice Johnson

Biography: Alice Johnson. "I was brought up to be afraid of horses, because my mother was afraid of horses. Two weeks after buying our first horse, I invited a friend to ride and the first thing she said after she saw me handle the horse was, "You can tell you have been around horses most of your life," and I replied, "Yes, a total of two weeks." I was a leader of the Hoofbeats 4-H club in Wakefield, Rhode Island, for a number of years, and spent hours making riding jackets for my tall, thin son and daughter. I started out as a bookkeeper and bought the grocery business from my employers when they wanted to retire. I retired from that in 1951 when my first son was born. I stay busy now that the three children have flown the coop by quilting, knitting, sewing and painting. I am still active in 4-H, helping to raise money for their state program. I was inducted into the Rhode Island 4-H volunteer hall of fame in 1999 and I am a young 81-year-old lady!"

Chapter Ten
Follow Those Dreams

My life With Horses

I can't remember a time in my life, even back in kindergarten, when I didn't love horses. As soon as I could read, I devoured everything in the library that had a horse on its cover. Even in the midst of my adolescent life, when Elvis domineered the walls in my bedroom...there were still the horse statues (about 50 of them), the books and photos. Every Saturday morning I would be glued to the TV set watching *Roy Rogers*, or *My Friend Flicka,* or *Fury* or *Gene Autry and Champion* and of course, *The Lone Ranger*. I knew someday I would have my very own horse; little did I know it wouldn't be for about another 20 years.

I lived in a small apartment in a small town, with access to the open spaces of New Jersey. My parents struggled through the '40s and '50s after the war, but they were able to give me the greatest gift of my life – riding lessons. The week would drag by until I could jump into dad's car for the 15-minute ride to the riding stable. We couldn't afford a lot at that time, but somehow my parents managed and before long I belonged to the riding club. We would do early morning trail rides and years later I progressed into overnight campouts with horses tied out for the night. I loved it. I learned so much about horses then; I studied them and they studied me, too. I knew then that my life would always revolve around horses; it was meant to be.

I'll never forget the promise I made to myself at the tender age of 13, one night at the local county fair. There was a horse show going on in the center ring and the stables all around were bustling with activity. I watched girls my age groom, saddle their horses and go into the arena to be judged. I saw the biggest grin on their faces when they got their ribbons, their families crowded around, so proud of their accomplishments. I wanted that too. Add to that atmosphere the warm summer night, tree frogs singing, the sweet smell of freshly-cut hay and the heavenly aroma of a freshly shampooed horse. This picture would be forever embedded in my mind. Someday I would accomplish this, but I had no idea that I would succeed beyond a county fair level.

Although my high school days were busy with studies – and of course, boys – I could always find time for a ride. My favorite horse was Cheyenne, black with a white snip on his nose. He was special to me because he seemed to like me the most of all the club members. The owner, after much pleading, finally let me ride him exclusively.

We rode Western at that club, did barrel racing, pole bending, etc. I got my "seat" and learned so much.

Then I graduated and got a job. I needed a car for work. Mom and Dad said they would help me get one, but about the same time I found out Cheyenne was for sale. I tossed and turned many nights … but it was more logical to get the car. That was one of the saddest times of my life up to that point.

In the late '70s, my husband Bob and I and our two young sons moved to Randolph and built a home on about five acres of property, with all kinds of riding trails behind our house. So it wasn't long before I set up the barn and bought my first horse, a gelding from out West named Tom. Before long, I had boarders and developed some lasting friendships. (That's the bonus of hanging with horses; horse people are just a friendly bunch.)

As the years went by, I acquired an Arabian mare that was bred and started the next phase of my life with horses. A cute colt was the result. I read and studied how to raise a colt and halter-break and break him to ride. About two and a half years later I stepped into the stirrup and sat on his back for the first time, urged him forward, and we were a huge success. I wasn't a bit scared. I don't think he was, either. I still had that dream in the back of my mind, but knew it would have to wait until I had more time and money. Showing Arabians is an expensive hobby.

Progress made my horse life here at home change. Housing developments behind our property and traffic on the road made it impossible to get to the power lines to ride into neighboring towns. It was the end of an era. As a result, I sold the horses I had through a wonderful friend, Barbara, and purchased my first show horse. Was he ever impressive! Almost 16 hands – large for an Arabian – dark dappled gray, three and a half years old. Boy, was I a happy lady. Now 38, my vision as a young teenager riding up to the judge to collect my blue ribbon was now a virtual possibility. All I had to do was learn to ride professionally, which I did faithfully with the wonderful trainer, Liz. The horse, Tyger El Tigro (Tigger), well, he knew what to do already.

He was the smoothest riding horse ever and no matter where we showed, it never failed that people would come up to me and say, "I love your horse, he's beautiful." Even judges would approach me after a class and say he was a special horse, had a great way of going, he floated. I floated riding him! My dream came true many times over to due to Tigger and I'll be forever in his debt. Trunks full of trophies and ribbons helped me realize a childhood dream at the ripe old age of 38. I thought I would see him live out his life with me, put my grandchildren up on his back for a ride, always be there in the morning for his apple, but fate had a different road for him. He passed away at the young age of 11.

Tigger is with me always. He and I were a match made in heaven and that's where I'll find him once again

Melissa (Perry) Ginsberg

Biography: Melissa (Perry) Ginsberg. Melissa called Morris Plains, New Jersey, her home for the first 20 years of her life. It was there that she began her infatuation with horses. After post-high school bank employment, Melissa married Bob and raised children, Marc and Jason, in the open spaces of Randolph, New Jersey. There she excelled in real estate, bred Arabian horses and acquired Tyger, a winning show horse.

Her goal is to share this love of horses with her grandchildren. "Involvement with horses at a young age is a great benefit to the children. I want them to learn to appreciate how wonderful and endearing these animals are", says Melissa.

The Cow Pens

The cow pens are quiet now, except for the occasional cry from a dry cow trying to locate her companions. As I walk through the pens late in the evening to open the gate for my horse to go out to the pasture, I can still see and hear the day's events just as though they were still going on. It's hard to believe how chilly it had been this mid-April morning at 5:00 a.m., compared to how warm and humid it is now.

As the cowboys fed and saddled their horses for the day's work, it was easy to feel how good we all felt even though we were tired from the day before. While the barn lights illuminated the yard, I was privileged to witness the skill and care each man gave his horse. The dogs sitting beside me, we watched as each horse displayed his or her version of just how good they felt. Stinky tiptoed in like a cat, the bay filly was bucking and Willow just stood there with big eyes. The barnyard was full of youthful energy, mostly on the part of the horses. As the horses settled and the men rode off with the dogs trotting eagerly beside them, I watched them ride into the morning darkness until I could no longer see them. I peered at the clock and estimated how much time I had to clean stalls, freshen water buckets, hang hay nets. I dug in to do my chores.

In a little while, as the biggest, reddest sun rose over the pens on the eastern horizon, I heard them, faint at first, then louder. Cows bellowing, whips cracking, dogs barking. I knew they were coming, and soon.

155

Presently I could see the lead cows, and through the many bovine bodies and dust, the men. Confident and determined, horses side-by-side like the best football defense line, they brought the cattle into the pens. It felt like a dream, from 100 years ago.

I realize that it's almost time to take my son to the school bus stop and I leave the barn. Happy to see his still sleepy face, we spend a little time talking while I make his breakfast. He likes to help his dad when he can, but this morning he waves to him from the truck as we drive by. *There's your bus. OK mom, see ya this afternoon ... love you.* And I watch him go.

Back in the pens, I go to the hopper to help keep a steady stream of cows and calves to be sorted. Cows one way, bulls and heifer calves another. More dust, more noise, and flies. My horse hates flies; I forgot to spray her and she's letting me know it. She's not being very cooperative today, but we manage to get the job done. With a thankful look from my horse, I spray her and put her in the stall for a while. I wonder what the cowboys would have done years ago? I bet their horses had tough skin, and I laughed to myself.

Hey! Come on, let's get started is what I hear and I run to my post beside the squeeze chute. Two shots, intramuscular and sub-q, I am told, and use the push pole if they get balky. One after the other the cows come. Some are willing, and others don't even want to think of going into the noisy squeeze chute. After a few cows, we all get into a rhythm and it's really amazing to see how quickly we get all these cows worked. I feel privileged to work side-by-side with these men and they make it easy for me, too, with their respect and confidence, but it's still loud, hot and dirty and I have cow poop all over me.

After lunch, we go back to the pens to castrate the young males, they have been without their mothers for a few hours now and they are less than cooperative. We get run over and kicked some, then the calves go back to the cows and we put them all back in their pasture. They soon forget about us, but we remember them for days.

Back at the barn we sit and reflect on the day. Part of it was funny, part of it serious. I'm tired, the horses are calling for supper and our own tummies remind us that it's that time as well. After the horses are fed and tucked in, I go to the bus stop and collect my son. He had a good day at school and tells me they didn't do much today. I just look over at him and smile; my day was good, too.

With the supper dishes washed and finally clean myself, my son is ready for bed. He didn't have homework so he wants to turn in early. After he says his prayers, I give him a kiss and tell him how much I love him. *Good night! Sleep tight!* we say, almost at the same time, and laugh.

My husband sits at his computer, typing in the cow numbers and stats. I rub his shoulders and give him a kiss goodnight on his cheek, and he kisses me back. I honestly can't remember my head even touching the pillow and the alarm clock is blinking *its morning* again...

Mona Malone

Biography: Mona Malone. "I am married and have two boys, Justin, 18, and Clint, 13. We have four horses, three dogs and three cats. We live on the Anclote River Ranch (3400 acres) located in Odessa, Florida, where my husband, Kim, is the ranch foreman. The ranch, steeped in Starkey family history, was mainly a commercial cow/calf operation and has now branched out to the ecotourism industry where we give guided tours. We are involved in barrel racing, reining, working cow horses, and starting and training our own colts. I thank God for the beauty around me and the gift of writing!"

A Dream Trots Into Reality

Hooves touched the soft earth in a rhythmic beat, wooden cart wheels creaked, and family voices played tag with the warm June breeze – a page from the annual ride-a-thon at Twin Peaks ranch.

A halo of blond hair framed the tanned face of my four-year-old grandson. "Grandma, is it almost my turn?"

"Almost. When the horse stops and the woman calls us, I'll help you into the cart." Tucked into my hand, his fingers gently tapped my palm. "Grandma?"

"Yes Sam."

"Do they step on a brake to stop?"

"No, honey, it's like when you're horseback riding with Grandpa or me and we pull back on the reins…"

"And I say *whoa*."

"That's right."

And then, Sam's long-awaited moment. I watched horse and cart, Sam and driver, move in a large circle. Puffed clouds drifted across their blue arena. Memories of a young girl in love with horses flowed through my mind. Sam waved and smiled as the cart rolled to a stop.

"Did you see how fast I went?"

I nodded. "You looked great."

We thanked the tall, soft-spoken woman and turned to leave. "Aren't you going for ride?" she asked.

"I thought you were only taking children," I said.

"Anyone can come, just climb aboard." Her smile and invitation was all I needed. Sam's mother walked him back to the bleachers. I stepped into one of my dreams.

My fascination with the cart and horse began as a young girl once I saw my first sulky race at the fair. "Someday" was a mantra that tugged at my heart every time I saw one of those races. And now... almost there!

"Would you like to drive?" My heart quickened. "Really?"

"Sure." She handed me the reins. Exhilaration swept through me. It wasn't a sulky race, but I was driving a trotter at a marvelous two-beat gait! I wasn't prepared for what happened next. Anyone who has felt that beautiful shift into a oneness with their activity or the innate connection with an animal knows the electric charge that flowed through my hands and body. I shivered with pure joy!

"You are a natural," she said. I was hooked!

Around the bend of my dream was another exciting chapter. My husband and I joined others volunteering for the Whitewater Therapeutic Riding and Recreation Association in our community. I obtained my NARAH Instructor's Certification and am currently working toward certification as a driving instructor. What a joy to extend the invitation for others to experience the pleasure of driving a horse and cart. Maybe another young girl's dream will trot into reality.

Margaret C. Hevel

Biography: Margaret C. Hevel. " I was a consultant and reviewer for educational materials with Marsh Film Co., Kendall School for the Deaf, WA. D.C. and Gallaudet College. As a Nurse Health Educator, I was founder and director of a child abuse/neglect prevention program. I presented at workshops, seminars and conferences in the northwest and nationally. My poems and short stories have been published in magazines and newspapers. I have written four novels. The last one was in collaboration with my daughter and I am a driving instructor with the WTRRA Equine Therapeutic Program."